The 85 Questions You Ask When You Begin a Relationship With God

The 85 Questions You Ask When You Begin a Relationship With God

Chris Palmer

LIGHT OF TODAY
PUBLISHING

ISBN-13: 9781542905244
ISBN-10: 1542905249
Library of Congress Control Number: 2017901682
CreateSpace Independent Publishing Platform
North Charleston, South Carolina

To those asking questions…

Keep on asking, and you will receive what you ask for. Keep on seeking, and you will find. Keep on knocking, and the door will be opened to you. For everyone who asks, receives. Everyone who seeks, finds. And to everyone who knocks, the door will be opened.
—MATTHEW 7:7-8

Contents

Introduction

Dear Friend—
Beginning a relationship with God through Jesus Christ is the greatest choice anyone can make. This is because a personal connection to the Lord produces marvelous transformation — even the toughest criminals are changed into radiant and lovely human beings when they find Christ. I have seen it happen over and over again. Jesus is the hope of humanity — he is what we are all searching for, whether we realize it or not.

Upon starting a relationship with the Lord, you may have *some* questions or even *a lot* of questions. But questions are good. Questions indicate interest, a drive to learn, and a desire to increase knowledge and understanding. They are tools, actually. They are a flashlight to help you find what you are looking for and a key to help you unlock where you haven't been. In fact, it would be concerning if you *didn't* have questions.

We should take advantage of the questions we have and use them to grow. For instance, look at children. According to Warren Berger, author of *A More Beautiful Question,* they will ask about 40,000 questions between the ages of 2 and 5.[1] And this should be applauded. Their inquisitiveness leads them to the information they are seeking; they slowly began to take control of their world, and they grow up. In this way, your relationship with Christ is much the same.

At Light of Today, we value your questions because God values your thinking. He gave you a mind and expects you to use it to discover more about him. Therefore, it is our desire to assist with this. In this book, we have laid out questions that are commonly asked by people who are beginning their relationship with God. And not only have we provided the questions, but we have given to you the best possible answers from God's Word, the Bible, in a manner that is easy to read, remember, and repeat.

Of course, answers lead to further questions, as you will discover while reading. But be encouraged: further questions lead to further knowledge. And further knowledge deepens your faith in Christ. This is what growth looks like. So esteem your questions because they will make you mature.

---

1 Warren Berger. *A More Beautiful Question.* (New York, New York: Bloomsbury, 2016), p. 40.

May God give you more and more grace and peace as you grow in your knowledge of God and Jesus our Lord.
—2 PETER 1:2

Maranatha
Chris Palmer

CHAPTER 1

What Does God Think of Me?

We are first going to deal with questions that concern *you*. You are always on your own mind, aren't you? So, this is a perfect place to begin. If we begin anywhere else, you might hurry through the questions, wondering when we are going to get to more personal questions. But that's fine; that's being human. God actually has a lot to say about you. So, he is glad we are starting here too.

Question #1: Does God like me?

The majority of people who struggle with the thought of having a relationship with God believe that God doesn't like them very much. As a person once said, "God and I have a good relationship: I hate him and he hates me." Have you ever felt that God hates you?

The truth is that God doesn't hate you. Sure, you might have had a very rough life up to this point, but this is not because God hates you. God likes you — in fact, God loves you! Let's look at what the Bible says:

> *For this is how God loved the world: He gave his one and only Son, so that everyone who believes in him will not perish but have eternal life.*
> *—John 3:16*

> *But God is so rich in mercy, and he loved us so much, that even though we were dead because of our sins, he gave us life when he raised Christ from the dead. (It is only by God's grace that you have been saved!)*
> *—Ephesians 2:4-5*

Whether you realize it or not, God has been your biggest fan throughout life. He has believed in you when nobody else has. Even if you have given up on yourself, God still has high hopes for you. If God had a smart phone, your picture would be his wallpaper. And that is the first thing you need to know.

Question #2: So God likes me even though I have done bad things to people?

He does. God's love is unconditional: there is nothing you can do to make him love you less, and there is nothing you can do to make him love you more. This means that God's love is perfect: it is total, full, and complete. And God has set that love upon you.

When you feel that God doesn't love you because of what you have done to people, that is actually *you* not loving *you*. We are miserable people without the love of God. But God did something to end our misery; he took the initiative to deliver us from it. Look at what the Bible says:

> *But God showed his great love for us by sending Christ*
> *to die for us while we were still sinners.*
> —*ROMANS 5:8*

The key words here are *while we were still sinners*. Our sin didn't keep God from loving us, and it sure didn't stop him from helping us. The fact is, we were bad people when God decided to step in and help us. There has to be something about us that God likes in order for him to do something like that.

Question #3: Something bad happened to me. Is that God punishing me for all the bad I have done?

It is common for human beings to associate God with punishment. Culture is filled with expressions of a deity mercilessly striking mortals for their insubordination. And this is one area where the God of the Bible differs so greatly from other so-called gods: the Lord is very compassionate. He is not quick to punish for wrongdoing. This is because God has the heart of a kind father. Look at what the Bible says:

> *The Lord is compassionate and merciful, slow to get angry,*
> *and filled with unfailing love. The Lord is like a father to his*
> *children, tender and compassionate to those who fear him. For he*
> *knows how weak we are; he remembers we are only dust.*
> —*PSALM 103:8, 13-14*

Though bigger and stronger, God does not rule with an iron fist. He leads with compassion and mercy. He understands our struggles and he empathizes with us.

Like any good father, the Lord shows paternal care towards us. Part of being a good parent means showing discipline. There *are* times where God *does* correct us. The Bible says:

> *For the Lord disciplines those he loves, and he*
> *punishes each one he accepts as his child.*
> —*HEBREWS 12:6*

Discipline means to direct, teach, and instruct a child who is headed toward maturity. *Punish* means to correct through pain. This might sound harsh, but when we consider that a loving father is administering this correction, we hardly see a picture of a God that is throwing lightning bolts at us to teach us a lesson. Instead, we see a Father who is using the choices we made to teach us a lesson. And that may even mean allowing us to *experience the consequences* of our decisions so that we can learn from them. So, if you make a choice and experience pain from that choice, ask God what he is teaching you. Then commit to him you will not repeat the same thing.

With that said, it should bring you relief to know that God doesn't fire off a random chain of bad events in your life because you have done something wrong. God won't make a shelf fall on your head, cause you to get into a car accident, or put cancer on you. Tragic things like this happen because:

- Satan caused it (John 10:10).
- Persistent disobedience keeps us out of God's will where he cannot protect us (Psalm 91).
- Human error.

The Lord will always warn us ahead of time before tragedy strikes and he will try to keep us from it. He is a good father and always has our best well-being in mind.

Question #4: Why do I feel guilty all of the time? Is this how God wants me to feel?

The majority of people feel guilty about something. In many cases, that guilt is unwarranted. A person may feel guilty for going on vacation, enjoying life, and having a good time. Some people feel guilty for saying *no*. Others feel guilty for the misfortunes of others. And many people feel guilty and have no idea why. Plenty of people who deal with guilt just accept that it is how God wants them to feel, so they live and die with it. But guilt is not from God.

The moment a person repents for their sin and places their faith in Jesus Christ, their sin is forgiven — even the most reprehensible wrongdoings. Look at what the Bible says:

Repent therefore and be converted, that your sins may be blotted out,
so that times of refreshing may come from the presence of the Lord
—ACTS 3:19

Do you not know that the unrighteous will not inherit the kingdom of God?
Do not be deceived. Neither fornicators, nor idolaters, nor adulterers, nor
homosexuals, nor sodomites, nor thieves, nor covetous, nor drunkards, nor
revilers, nor extortioners will inherit the kingdom of God. And such were
some of you. But you were washed, but you were sanctified, but you were
justified in the name of the Lord Jesus and by the Spirit of our God.
—1 CORINTHIANS 6:9-11

At this point, there is no reason to feel guilty. And God certainly doesn't want you to feel guilty since it steals the joy he died for you to have. So if guilt isn't coming from God, where is it coming from? The Bible gives two sources:

- Satan: The Bible says that Satan is the accuser. To accuse means to bring charges against; it means to allege guilt. Satan does this so that we forget about God's forgiveness and stay stuck in our past.

> *For the accuser of our brothers and sisters has been thrown down to*
> *earth—the one who accuses them before our God day and night.*
> *—REVELATION 12:10B*

- A weak conscience: A weak conscience refers to a conscience that believes something is wrong when it is, in fact, not. This is discussed in 1 Corinthians 8. In this chapter, some Christians felt that eating a certain kind of meat was wrong. Therefore, they didn't eat it because it would cause them guilt. However, according to God, there was nothing wrong with eating this particular kind of meat. These Christians were just uninformed. An uninformed Christian is a Christian who doesn't understand the freedom that they have in Christ. And when we don't understand the freedom we have in Christ, we may end up feeling guilty for things that are perfectly fine to do, like going on vacation or saying *no* when people ask us to do things that we don't want to do or can't do.

Question #5: Am I worthy enough to have a relationship with God?

When we live with guilt, we feel like we are not good enough to have a relationship with God. We wonder, *Why does God want anything to do with me?* This guilty thinking causes hopelessness and despair. Then, it becomes offensive to hear that God desires to be close to us. But the Scripture tells us that we are, in fact, worthy. Our worthiness is not the result of anything we have done. It is the result of what Christ has done for us. Look at what the Bible says:

> *For He made Him who knew no sin to be sin for us, that*
> *we might become the righteousness of God in Him.*
> *—2 CORINTHIANS 5:21*

Righteousness means to live up to God's standard of right. Though we haven't, God regards us as though we have, because God sees Christ's righteousness as belonging to us. Notice:

> *I no longer count on my own righteousness through obeying the law; rather, I*
> *become righteous through faith in Christ. For God's way of making us right with*

himself depends on faith. I want to know Christ and experience the mighty power
that raised him from the dead. I want to suffer with him, sharing in his death
—PHILIPPIANS 3:9B-10

Christ's righteousness gives us a position of favor with God, where we can draw near to him with confidence and make requests.

So then, since we have a great High Priest who has entered heaven, Jesus the
Son of God, let us hold firmly to what we believe. This High Priest of ours
understands our weaknesses, for he faced all of the same testings we do, yet he
did not sin. So let us come boldly to the throne of our gracious God. There we
will receive his mercy, and we will find grace to help us when we need it most.
—HEBREWS 4:14-16

As a result, we can:

- Be certain that we aren't a bother to God.
- Know that God welcomes us into his presence.
- Pray with confidence and expect God to hear us.

Because some realize they haven't earned this kind of favor with God, they think, *How is this fair?* But our relationship with God cannot be earned: it is a result of God's loving grace. He just wants us to accept it and receive it.

God saved you by his grace when you believed. And you can't take
credit for this; it is a gift from God. Salvation is not a reward for
the good things we have done, so none of us can boast about it.
—EPHESIANS 2:8-9

CHAPTER 2
What Should I Think About God?

Since we have discovered what God thinks about us, it now makes sense for us to find out what God wants us to think about him. The vast majority of people who want nothing to do with God have misunderstandings about him that are not consistent with how God has revealed himself to humanity. Though God is an inexhaustible subject, let's at least ask a few questions that will help us learn more about him and his goodness.

Question #6: How do I know God exists?

This is a fair question and we have all asked it before. It is important to start by saying that faith in God requires a break from relying strictly on rationalism. Rationalism is the theory that reason, not experience, is the foundation of certainty. Reason is a rationalist's authority and they depend on it solely. Being the case, a rationalist looks to science for enlightenment because science is based on what can be proved with the eye. At this point, science hasn't given them what they are looking for to prove that God exists. But, on the other hand, science hasn't given them what they are looking for to disprove God exists. The best a rationalist can do is to say, *We don't know if he exists or not.*

But is rationalism the only way to discover truth? According to the majority of the world who believe in God, it's not. People of faith believe in the supernatural — that which is above studies of modern science. Just because we can't find God through a telescope, does that mean he can't be found? Maybe we need a better telescope. In other words, science doesn't have all the answers because there is more than meets the eye.

As Christians, we believe God has revealed himself to us in three ways:

- The inner desire to know God: Within every human, there is a deep witness that we have a Creator. We also have a longing to know that Creator. The Scripture tells us that this witness makes God's existence obvious to us.

> *They know the truth about God because he has made it obvious to them.*
> *—ROMANS 1:19*

Denying the obvious existence of God is a result of irrational thinking that comes from living a life of sin and pride.

> *For they brag about their evil desires; they praise the*
> *greedy and curse the Lord. The wicked are too proud to*
> *seek God. They seem to think that God is dead.*
> —PSALM 10:3-4

- Nature: A universe with order and harmony suggests that it was designed intelligently, not just by random chance. When we consider the excellence, skill, and detail of life and nature, we are led to believe that a Creator has done all this with purpose.

> *The heavens proclaim the glory of God. The skies display*
> *his craftsmanship. Day after day they continue to speak;*
> *night after night they make him known.*
> —PSALM 19:1-2

- Scripture (special revelation): Special revelation is how God has revealed himself to mankind, supernaturally. It includes miracles, signs, wonders, and of course, the Bible. God inspired the authors of Scripture to record his message for mankind. Everything he desires for mankind to know at this point has been placed into Scripture and remains a sure testimony that he not only exists, but is participating in the ongoing purposes of humanity.

> *All Scripture is inspired by God and is useful to teach us what is*
> *true and to make us realize what is wrong in our lives. It corrects*
> *us when we are wrong and teaches us to do what is right.*
> —2 TIMOTHY 3:16

Question 7: Can I really know God; aren't his ways mysterious?

It's a mistake to call God *mysterious*. Mysterious means difficult or impossible to understand. Saying this casts a poor light on God — it makes him seem distant and aloof from his creation. That's exactly the opposite of how God wants us to think about him. No, he is actively engaging and manifesting himself to humanity. Notice what the Bible says:

> *That is what the Scriptures mean when they say, "No eye has seen, no ear*
> *has heard, and no mind has imagined what God has prepared for those*
> *who love him." But it was to us that God revealed these things by his Spirit.*
> *For his Spirit searches out everything and shows us God's deep secrets.*
> —1 CORINTHIANS 2:9-10

God has revealed to us what he is like, how he thinks, what his desire is for us, how we can be close to him, and what he expects of us. And more than this, God has invited us to know him personally. In Jeremiah it says:

> *This is what the Lord says: "Don't let the wise boast in their wisdom,*
> *or the powerful boast in their power, or the rich boast in their riches.*
> *But those who wish to boast should boast in this alone: that they*
> *truly know me and understand that I am the Lord who demonstrates*
> *unfailing love and who brings justice and righteousness to the earth,*
> *and that I delight in these things. I, the Lord, have spoken!*
> *—JEREMIAH 9:23-24*

Many of the things that people say they don't understand about God could and would be understood through having a personal fellowship with him. Through this special fellowship we *experience* God's thoughts and ways. And the more we experience, the less mysterious he becomes.

Therefore, instead of calling God mysterious, we can say that he is unfathomable. This means that we will never be able to *fully* know everything about him because God is so vast and great. The Scripture tells us this:

> *Great is the Lord, and greatly to be praised; and his greatness is unsearchable.*
> *—PSALM 145:3*

Yet, just because he is vast and great does not mean we can't know anything about him or shouldn't try. God desires for us to know him; he has made plain many things about himself to us, and he will continue doing so throughout eternity. But we don't have to wait until eternity to begin. We can start right now!

Question #8: Is Jesus God?

Yes. Absolutely. The Scripture is very clear that Jesus Christ is God along with the Father and the Holy Spirit (known as the Trinity). Here are some of the indisputable proofs from Scripture that Jesus is God:

- The word *God* is ascribed to Jesus often:

> *While we look forward with hope to that wonderful day when the*
> *glory of our great God and Savior, Jesus Christ, will be revealed.*
> *—TITUS 2:13*

- The word *Lord* is ascribed to Jesus often. In referring to Jesus, *Lord* means God and Creator, as the term was used in the Septuagint to refer to *YHWH* (Yahweh or Jehovah):

The Savior—yes, the Messiah, the Lord—has been
born today in Bethlehem, the city of David!
—LUKE 2:11

- Jesus forgave sins. This is something only sovereign God can do:

  Seeing their faith, Jesus said to the paralyzed man, "My child, your sins are
  forgiven." But some of the teachers of religious law who were sitting there thought
  to themselves, "What is he saying? This is blasphemy! Only God can forgive sins!"
  —MARK 2:5-7

- Jesus died and rose from the dead: He had the power to lay his life down and to take it back up:

  "The Father loves me because I sacrifice my life so I may take it back
  again. 18 No one can take my life from me. I sacrifice it voluntarily.
  For I have the authority to lay it down when I want to and also to
  take it up again. For this is what my Father has commanded."
  —JOHN 10:17-18

- Jesus is worthy to be worshipped:

  Therefore, God elevated him to the place of highest honor and gave him
  the name above all other names, that at the name of Jesus every knee
  should bow, in heaven and on earth and under the earth, and every
  tongue declare that Jesus Christ is Lord, to the glory of God the Father.
  —PHILIPPIANS 2:9-11

Question #9: How can God be three in one?

Some are critical of Christianity because Christians worship God the Father, the Son, and the Holy Spirit — the Trinity. The term *Trinity* means that God is three persons and yet one God. Though it may be a challenge for our human minds to comprehend, this is precisely what the Scripture teaches.

The Trinity can be summed up in three statements[2]:

- God is three persons: The Father is not the Son, the Father is not the Holy Spirit, the Son is not the Holy Spirit.

---

2 Wayne Grudem. *Systematic Theology: An Introduction to Biblical Doctrine.* (Grand Rapids, MI: Zondervan, 2000), 231.

May the grace of the Lord Jesus Christ, the love of God, and
the fellowship of the Holy Spirit be with you all.
—2 CORINTHIANS 13:14

- Each is fully God: The Father is fully God (Genesis 1:1), the Son is fully God (Titus 2:13), and the Holy Spirit is fully God (Matthew 28:19; Acts 5:3-4).
- There is one God: God is only one being. There are not three Gods, just one (Exodus 15:11; Romans 3:30).

Both the Testaments teach the same:

- Old Testament: In the story of creation, Genesis teaches a number of persons in the Godhead.

Then God said, "Let us make human beings in our image, to be like us."
—GENESIS 1:26A

The *us* in this passage implies that more than one person is involved. But the Old Testament also teaches that God is one being.

Hear, O Israel: The Lord our God is one Lord
—DEUTERONOMY 6:4

- New Testament: When Jesus was baptized, all three persons of the Godhead were represented.

And Jesus, when he was baptized, went up straightway out of the water:
and, lo, the heavens were opened unto him, and he saw the Spirit of
God descending like a dove, and lighting upon him: And lo a voice from
heaven, saying, This is my beloved Son, in whom I am well pleased.
—MATTHEW 3:16-17

Here we see the Son being baptized in water, the Holy Spirit descending upon him, and the Father speaking from Heaven. But the New Testament also teaches that God is one being:

You say you have faith, for you believe that there is one God. Good for you!
—JAMES 2:19A

The Trinity is an example of God's unsearchable vastness. It is difficult for us as human beings to fully understand this. God understands our questions; he shows compassion for us because we can't wrap our heads around it. Nevertheless, he is pleased when we receive what his Word teaches by faith.

Question #10: How can a loving God put people in Hell?

This question seems to hang up even the sincerest of people who are seeking God. On one hand they are told that God is loving and good, yet on the other hand they are told that God will send those who don't trust in him to Hell — a miserable place of torment, punishment, and suffering. To many, this seems cruel, mean, inconsistent, and even unfair. Some Christians are even embarrassed to talk about it.

But Jesus taught this. He said that Hell is a punishment for those who reject him. Notice:

> *Then the King will turn to those on the left and say, 'Away with you, you cursed ones, into the eternal fire prepared for the devil and his demons.*
> *—MATTHEW 25:41*

Jesus was very clear that, though Hell was created *for* Satan, those who reject God will end up there *with* Satan.

This is because God is holy (1 Peter 1:16). This means that God is perfect, without flaw, and the standard of all that is good. Sinning against God is a heinous crime — far more heinous than twisted human minds can realize. Therefore, how can humans suggest what their punishment for sin should be when they can't properly understand how great a crime it is to offend a holy God?

God is also a righteous judge (Psalm 7:9). Righteous means that God will always do what is right. And this means punishing wickedness because it is the right thing to do. Punishing wickedness is the right thing to do because:

- It brings justice.
- It vindicates the innocent.
- If God didn't punish wickedness, people would have great incentive to be as wicked as they wanted to be in this life.

Yet, in spite of all this, God is love (1 John 4:8). He doesn't desire that anyone go to Hell. Look what the Bible says:

> *The Lord isn't really being slow about his promise, as some people think. No, he is being patient for your sake. He does not want anyone to be destroyed, but wants everyone to repent.*
> *—2 PETER 3:9*

God sent Jesus to bear our guilt and die for our sins. He was our *propitiation*. This means that his death appeased God's wrath and, as a result, God became favorable to us:

> *Whom God hath set forth to be a propitiation through faith*
> *in his blood, to declare his righteousness for the remission of*
> *sins that are past, through the forbearance of God*
> —ROMANS 3:25

Now, anyone who places their trust in Christ will escape God's wrath and receive God's favor:

> *Much more then, being now justified by his blood, we*
> *shall be saved from wrath through him.*
> —ROMANS 5:9

That God has sacrificed his only Son to save us from the penalty of our heinous offenses toward him, far exceeds fairness; it means that God is gracious and merciful. Because of this we should be eternally thankful rather than to accuse him of being unfair.

Question #11: Doesn't everyone serve the same God whom they call by a different name?

God is the word used to describe the Supreme Being in the universe. However, just because the various religions of the world use the same word does not mean that their idea of who or what God is is the same. The only way to determine if two people are talking about the same God is to compare their descriptions. If there are too many significant differences, then it should be clear that they are not referring to the same God and, therefore, aren't worshipping or serving the same God.

For instance, when comparing *Allah* from the Quran to *Jehovah* from the Bible, it is very clear that they are not they same. When comparing *Shiva* from Hinduism to the *Holy Spirit* from Christianity, there is a major difference. When comparing *Zeus* to *Jesus,* there couldn't be more of a contrast.

It's not safe to assume that someone is serving Christ just because they refer to God. Until we hear what they believe about God, we cannot be sure.

Question #12: Why does God allow suffering and evil?

What this question is really asking is, *How can God be all-powerful and all-loving when, at the same time, suffering and evil exist?* Suffering and evil make it challenging for many to reconcile this. They reason that if God has all power and evil persists, then he isn't all loving but indifferent to human suffering. On the other hand, if he is all loving and evil persists, then he isn't all-powerful but helpless to do anything about it.

There are a few possible reasons that suffering and evil occur in spite of the fact that God is all-loving and all-powerful:

- God is allowing evil to run its course: God wants humanity to be certain that anything against his will causes suffering, pain, and death (Romans 3:23).
- God doesn't stop people from exercising their free will: People are free to chose right from wrong — God has given them that right — even if it causes suffering. However, since this is the case, wrongdoers will not be able to accuse God of being unjust when they are punished.
- Many humans wouldn't want God to stop *all* evil: If God put a stop to evil, he would have to put a stop to *all* evil. We desire to see the abolishment of rape, genocide, and catastrophe. But at the same time, many wouldn't want God abolish their pet sins, like bigotry, lying, gambling, or pride. To remove those, God would have to exert his will over man's. Therefore, evil persists because of man's free will.
- People turn to God in times of suffering: It is important to know that God is never the cause of suffering. Suffering is the result of human sin. Nevertheless, the Holy Spirit uses times of great suffering to lead men to realize the consequences of evil, the need for salvation, and the hope of the perfect world to come.

As Christians, we must be willing to trust that God is who his Word reveals him to be even when we don't quite understand why tragedy occurs. It's safe to say that we will go through life wondering why certain things happened, without really having an answer that satisfies us. In these instances, God asks us to have faith in him and trust that, in the grand scheme of things, all things are working together for our good. This is what the Bible teaches about our ultimate good:

> *And we know that God causes everything to work together for the good of*
> *those who love God and are called according to his purpose for them.*
> *—ROMANS 8:28*

When we seek God in times of suffering, he can give to us special faith in him and supernatural peace in our hearts without actually having an answer. This is God's desire for us when we are wrestling with suffering. Notice:

> *Then you will experience God's peace, which exceeds*
> *anything we can understand. His peace will guard your*
> *hearts and minds as you live in Christ Jesus.*
> *—PHILIPPIANS 4:7*

Question #13: Why should I try to be closer to God when I am already happy?

First, it isn't just about *you*. The Scripture tells us that our lives do not belong to us, they belong to God (or should). Notice:

> *You do not belong to yourself, for God bought you with a high price.*
> —1 CORINTHIANS 6:19B-20A

The purpose of our lives, then, is to honor God. One of the greatest ways that we can honor God is by honoring his invitation to know him. The King of the Universe has issued us a royal summons, inviting us to be close with him. The Bible mentions this:

> *And having chosen them, he called them to come to him. And having called them, he gave them right standing with himself. And having given them right standing, he gave them his glory.*
> —ROMANS 8:30

We accept this summons by loving the Lord with all of our heart, soul, mind, and strength, just as Jesus told us:

> *And you must love the Lord your God with all your heart, all your soul, all your mind, and all your strength.*
> —MARK 12:30

Our love for the Lord is demonstrated through seeking him with hunger and desire:

> *Search for the Lord and for his strength; continually seek him.*
> —PSALM 105:4

An apathetic attitude toward seeking the Lord reflects a listless love for God. It is a rejection to his invitation and is an offense to him. Consider how you may feel if you worked hard to prepare an event, excitedly invited your guests, and nobody bothered to show up. It would be painful and it would hurt. Jesus teaches us that this is how he feels when we reject *his* invitation:

> *Hearing this, a man sitting at the table with Jesus exclaimed, "What a blessing it will be to attend a banquet in the Kingdom of God!" Jesus replied with this story: "A man prepared a great feast and sent out many invitations. When the banquet was ready, he sent his servant to tell the guests, 'Come, the banquet is ready.' But they all began making excuses. One said, 'I have just bought a field and must inspect it. Please excuse me.' Another said, 'I have just bought five pairs of oxen, and I want to try them out. Please excuse me.' Another*

said, 'I just got married, so I can't come.' "The servant returned and told his master what they had said. His master was furious and said, 'Go quickly into the streets and alleys of the town and invite the poor, the crippled, the blind, and the lame.' After the servant had done this, he reported, 'There is still room for more.' So his master said, 'Go out into the country lanes and behind the hedges and urge anyone you find to come, so that the house will be full. For none of those I first invited will get even the smallest taste of my banquet.'
—*LUKE 14:15-24*

God is displeased with those who find "better" things to do than seek him. But those who do respond to his royal summons by seeking him will find God's blessing, eternal purpose, and everlasting life.

CHAPTER 3

Does God Want to Help Me?

The next thing we need to know is that God desires to help us. Contrary to what many believe, God is not your problem; he isn't out to get you or to make your life miserable. He has gone the distance to help you. And his will is that you will receive that help, right now.

Question 14: What has God saved me from?

It is common for Christians to refer to themselves as *saved*. This simply means that we are saved from the wrath of God, which is the consequence of sin. Notice:

> *Much more then, being now justified by his blood, we*
> *shall be saved from wrath through him.*
> *—ROMANS 5:9*

God is outraged by sin; he hates it intensely. And because he hates sin so intensely, it is the object of his wrath. Unless a person receives salvation, God's wrath will fall on them because they remain sinful. This is what God's Word says:

> *And anyone who believes in God's Son has eternal life.*
> *Anyone who doesn't obey the Son will never experience eternal*
> *life but remains under God's angry judgment.*
> *—JOHN 3:36*

But we don't have to remain sinful and we don't have to experience God's wrath. God sent Jesus to help us escape. This escape is known as *salvation*. We receive salvation when we hear God's Word, trust it with our heart, and confess it with our mouth. This alone saves us from Hell and eternal separation from God — it also brings us eternal life:

> *If you openly declare that Jesus is Lord and believe in your heart*
> *that God raised him from the dead, you will be saved. For it is*
> *by believing in your heart that you are made right with God,*
> *and it is by openly declaring your faith that you are saved.*
> *—ROMANS 10:9-10*

Question 15: If I do enough good things, will I go to Heaven?

It's popular to believe that if we do more good things than bad things then we are good people and will go to Heaven when we die. Yet, while it is good to do good things, the Bible doesn't teach that good works get us into Heaven. This means that we don't go to Heaven for things like:

- Spreading positivity.
- Paying it forward.
- Going to mass/church.
- Saying the Rosary.
- Helping the poor.
- Being nice people.
- Commemorating saints.
- Paying penance.

This might be shocking to discover, perhaps even disappointing for some. Yet, Jesus constantly rebuked religious leaders for teaching that God's grace comes from meeting religious demands. Trying to follow the man-made rules of religion to earn salvation doesn't bring liberty. It is burdensome, it brings frustration, and it doesn't please God. Jesus said this himself:

> *Then Jesus said to the crowds and to his disciples, "The teachers of*
> *religious law and the Pharisees are the official interpreters of the law of*
> *Moses. So practice and obey whatever they tell you, but don't follow their*
> *example. For they don't practice what they teach. They crush people with*
> *unbearable religious demands and never lift a finger to ease the burden...*
> *Everything they do is for show...What sorrow awaits you teachers of*
> *religious law and you Pharisees...Outwardly you look like righteous people,*
> *but inwardly your hearts are filled with hypocrisy and lawlessness.*
> *—MATTHEW 23:1-5A, 27A, 28*

What is pleasing to God is following his formula for eternal life: salvation by grace through faith. Grace is the unmerited favor of God. It's the result of his goodness. Though we were sinners, God extended salvation to us from his goodness and not our own, because we had none. Notice:

> But God showed his great love for us by sending Christ
> to die for us while we were still sinners.
> —ROMANS 5:8

The way we receive this salvation is through having faith in what Jesus has done for us:

> God saved you by his grace when you believed. And you can't take
> credit for this; it is a gift from God. Salvation is not a reward for
> the good things we have done, so none of us can boast about it.
> —EPHESIANS 2:8-9

So you see, good works do not *bring* salvation; only faith in God's grace does. Therefore, salvation is nothing we can earn — it's a gift.

Question 16: What is being "born again"?

Evangelical Christians use this term often. It refers to an inward, supernatural transformation of the heart by God. It means that God has filled our hearts with new life and that life overflows from within. And it isn't just any kind of life, it is God's divine life. In the most difficult situations and trying circumstances, this life shines forth from us and people can see Jesus living in us — because he is.

Jesus spoke about this transformation and told us that we all need to be born again. Notice:

> Jesus replied, "I tell you the truth, unless you are born
> again, you cannot see the Kingdom of God.
> —JOHN 3:3

Before we are born again, we are spiritually dead. This means:

- We are separated from God by our sins.
- We live in darkness, having no understanding of the things of God.
- We are miserable because of sin and separation from God.
- We are without eternal purpose.

The Scripture tells us this:

> Once you were dead because of your disobedience and your many sins. You
> used to live in sin, just like the rest of the world, obeying the devil—the

> *commander of the powers in the unseen world. He is the spirit at work in the hearts of those who refuse to obey God. All of us used to live that way, following the passionate desires and inclinations of our sinful nature. By our very nature we were subject to God's anger, just like everyone else.*
> —*EPHESIANS 2:1-3*

So when someone spiritually dead receives Jesus and is connected back to God, the Bible compares it to a rebirth. Christ comes to live inside of them and they become alive!

This supernatural transformation of the heart cannot be accomplished through religion, doing good, praying to saints, or any other act of piety. It can only come through faith in Christ. And it is not an option; Jesus said it is a must:

> *So don't be surprised when I say, 'You must be born again.*
> —*JOHN 3:7*

Question 17: Can I be certain that I will go to Heaven when I die?

Yes! You can be absolutely certain that you will be ushered into the presence of Jesus the moment you take your last breath. Look what the Bible says:

> *I have written this to you who believe in the name of the Son of God, so that you may know you have eternal life.*
> —*1 JOHN 5:13*

This confidence is one of the greatest blessings of being saved. God doesn't want you to walk through life, timid about your eternal destiny. He desires for you to have the peace that comes from knowing that your eternity is in his hands. God is good and he will keep his promise to you and ensure that, after death, you end up with him in Heaven. Jesus guaranteed us of this:

> *When everything is ready, I will come and get you, so that you will always be with me where I am.*
> —*JOHN 14:3*

Question 18: Am I going to have to wait in purgatory after death?

No. The Bible tells us that a Christian goes immediately into the presence of the Lord when they die:

> *Yes, we are fully confident, and we would rather be away from these earthly bodies, for then we will be at home with the Lord.*
> —*2 CORINTHIANS 5:8*

The apostle Paul said that there are only two options for a Christian: to live on this earth or to be with Christ in Heaven. He never taught purgatory or included it as even a slight possibility. Notice:

> *But if I live, I can do more fruitful work for Christ. So I really don't know which is better. I'm torn between two desires: I long to go and be with Christ, which would be far better for me. But for your sakes, it is better that I continue to live.*
> —*PHILIPPIANS 1:22-24*

According to *The Catholic Encyclopedia*, purgatory is "an intermediate state in which departed souls can atone for unforgiven sins before receiving their reward." It is a place where "the souls of those who have died in grace suffer...to cleanse one of imperfections, venial sins, faults, and to remit or do away with the temporal punishment due to mortal sins..."[3] Admittedly, however, *The Catholic Encyclopedia* says that "this state is not described in the teaching of the Church."[4] This means that it is not taught by Jesus or the apostles and it is not in Scripture.

And there is no wonder why it is not in Scripture: the Bible teaches that Jesus paid the price for all of our sins; he suffered so that we wouldn't have to. In other words, we can't atone for our own sins and we don't need to. He did it for us!

> *But he was pierced for our rebellion, crushed for our sins. He was beaten so we could be whole. He was whipped so we could be healed.*
> —*ISAIAH 53:5*

First, teaching purgatory incorrectly suggests that Christ's work was insufficient. And it wasn't. He atoned for us totally and completely and there's no need for us to make any additional contribution:

> *Unlike those other high priests, he does not need to offer sacrifices every day. They did this for their own sins first and then for the sins of the people. But Jesus did this once for all when he offered himself as the sacrifice for the people's sins.*
> —*HEBREWS 7:27*

Next, teaching purgatory creates fearful followers: fearful of missing mass, fearful of not giving penance, fearful of not going to confession. God doesn't desire his followers to serve him for fear of ending up in purgatory. He wants them to serve him out of thankfulness that his work was complete and Heaven awaits.

---

3 Robert Broderick. *The Catholic Encyclopedia*. (Nashville, TN: Thomas Nelson Inc., Publishers, 1976), 502.
4 Ibid.

Finally, teaching purgatory causes Christians to fear death. God doesn't want us to fear dying. He has delivered us from the fear of death and we should anticipate going home to be with the Lord with joy. Look:

> *Because God's children are human beings—made of flesh and blood—the Son also became flesh and blood. For only as a human being could he die, and only by dying could he break the power of the devil, who had the power of death. Only in this way could he set free all who have lived their lives as slaves to the fear of dying.*
> —*HEBREWS 2:14-15*

When a believer dies, their loved ones should be comforted knowing that they are with the Lord. Notice:

> *For Christ also hath once suffered for sins, the just for the unjust, that he might bring us to God.*
> —*1 PETER 3:18A*

The idea of purgatory steals this comfort and makes Christian funerals a time of bitter sorrow. But God hasn't called us to sorrow. He has called us to be hopeful in the face of death because he has defeated its ability to separate us from God:

> *But I would not have you to be ignorant, brethren, concerning them which are asleep, that ye sorrow not, even as others which have no hope.*
> —*1 THESSALONIANS 4:13*

Question 19: What does salvation include?

We sell ourselves short by thinking that the message of the Gospel is *accept Jesus so you can go to Heaven when you die.* Though going to Heaven is included, there's a lot more to it than that. It's a whole lot better, too!

Salvation includes the following:

- Regeneration: God imparts spiritual life to us. God makes us alive in Christ and gives us a new nature (being born again).

> *He saved us, not because of the righteous things we had done, but because of his mercy. He washed away our sins, giving us a new birth and new life through the Holy Spirit*
> —*TITUS 3:5*

- Justification: The legal act whereby God thinks of our sins as forgiven. He declares us righteous (to have right standing with him) because he regards us as having the perfect righteousness of Christ.

> *So just as sin ruled over all people and brought them to death, now*
> *God's wonderful grace rules instead, giving us right standing with*
> *God and resulting in eternal life through Jesus Christ our Lord.*
> *—ROMANS 5:21*

- Indwelling of the Holy Spirit: The Holy Spirit comes to take permanent residence inside of us.

> *He is the Holy Spirit, who leads into all truth. The world cannot receive*
> *him, because it isn't looking for him and doesn't recognize him. But you*
> *know him, because he lives with you now and later will be in you.*
> *—JOHN 14:17*

- Adoption: God makes us members of his family and gives to us an eternal inheritance.

> *So you have not received a spirit that makes you fearful slaves.*
> *Instead, you received God's Spirit when he adopted you as*
> *his own children. Now we call him, "Abba, Father."*
> *—ROMANS 8:15*

- Glorification: We receive glorified bodies when Christ returns. Our bodies will be entirely set free from the effects of the fall and brought into the state of perfection.

> *Just as everyone dies because we all belong to Adam, everyone who*
> *belongs to Christ will be given new life. But there is an order to*
> *this resurrection: Christ was raised as the first of the harvest; then*
> *all who belong to Christ will be raised when he comes back.*
> *—1 CORINTHIANS 15:22-23*

Salvation is a tremendous package of benefits that God has secured for us through Christ. It is a gift. And the proper way to receive a gift is with thankfulness. It blesses the heart of a gift-giver when they see the recipient of the gift enjoying what they got. For instance, if you bought a watch for someone, you would be blessed if you ran into them somewhere and found them wearing it. Likewise, God is blessed when he sees us enjoying the benefits of salvation. So, receive it. This blesses God's heart!

CHAPTER 4

Catholics and Evangelical Christians — What's the Difference?

It certainly is a task explaining the difference between Roman Catholicism and Evangelical Christianity. This is because it is a touchy subject and often ends in argument and offense. Therefore, to discuss it — especially as *briefly* as it is being done here — an open mind and a patient, non-combative attitude is required. Certainly, it is not our place to judge another person's heart or stipulate where they stand with God — only God can determine that. So we will focus on the practices and not on those who practice it. This is not to be taken personally. It only serves to provide a bit of truth about why Evangelical Christianity is closer to God's design for following Christ than Roman Catholicism is. This doesn't mean Catholics don't love Jesus or are not going to Heaven. It does mean, however, that following Christ the way born-again evangelicals do will provide a much deeper and more empowering relationship with the Lord.

Question 20: Are Catholics and Evangelical Christians on the same team?

First, a person's salvation is not determined by whether or not they identify as Catholic or Evangelical. Salvation and adoption into the family of God is determined by grace, through faith alone (Ephesians 2:8-9). This genuine relationship with the Lord comes about at conversion. Notice:

> *And said, Verily I say unto you, Except ye be converted, and become*
> *as little children, ye shall not enter into the kingdom of heaven.*
> —*MATTHEW 18:3*

Conversion means a change of lifestyle. It happens when a person becomes sorry for their sins, asks God for forgiveness, trusts Jesus to remove the burden of sin, and receives the indwelling presence of the Holy Spirit into their lives through the admission of Christ as Lord. Those who have done this are all on the same team — part of the same family, we should say — no matter what branch of Christianity they identify with. Catholics and Evangelicals who have had this same experience are brothers and sisters in Christ and should treat each other as such. This sort of unity is a witness to the world. Jesus said so:

Your love for one another will prove to the world that you are my disciples.
—JOHN 13:35

On the other hand, those who identify as Catholics or those who identify as Evangelicals — say, by attending mass or church — and have not sought God's forgiveness and have not been transformed by the Lord, are still lost and in need of salvation. An association with a church doesn't save us, only Jesus can.

That said, those who have converted and are Catholic practice their faith much differently than those who have converted and practice their faith evangelically. In this respect, they are different — very different. So whose practices are closer to Biblical Christianity? Evangelicals. This is because Evangelical Christianity places a far greater authority on the Bible than Catholicism does. Therefore, Evangelical practices are more *biblical* and closer to how the first century New Testament Christians followed Christ. It is through these biblical practices that we discover a deeper, more empowering relationship with the Lord.

Question 21: What authority does the Bible have?

God tells us that his Word is powerful and important. It is life-giving:

> *For the word of God is alive and powerful. It is sharper than the sharpest two-edged sword, cutting between soul and spirit, between joint and marrow. It exposes our innermost thoughts and desires.*
> *—HEBREWS 4:12*

This is because God's Word is inspired: God divinely influenced the human authors to write the perfect Word of God. Notice:

> *All Scripture is inspired by God and is useful to teach us what is true and to make us realize what is wrong in our lives. It corrects us when we are wrong and teaches us to do what is right.*
> *—2 TIMOTHY 3:16*

Because of this, Evangelicals believe that the Bible is the authority on faith and godly living. Using Scripture as authority was the practice of Christ and the apostles:

- Christ taught the Scriptures are authoritative (John 10:35).
- Christ taught that error comes from not knowing the Scriptures (Matthew 22:29).
- Christ rebuked those who didn't know the Scriptures (Matthew 22:29).
- James used Scripture to settle issues in the Church (Acts 15:16-18).
- Paul constantly appealed to Scripture (Romans 4:3; 2 Timothy 3:15).

- The Bereans tested all things by Scripture and their diligence was commended (Acts 17:11).
- Revelation tells us that those who read and hear the words of Scripture are blessed (Revelation 1:3).

For these reasons, Evangelicals place a high premium on reading, studying, and observing the Word of God. And this is why so many Evangelicals are biblically knowledgeable and literate. You will notice this when you enter an Evangelical church. People come in with their own personal Bibles, the pastor tells them what Scriptures to turn to, and the congregation follows along — they are learning the Bible. You might also notice that their Bibles are yellow with highlights and marked up with personal study notes. The people are being diligent to put God's Word in their hearts because God's Word imparts life.

Roman Catholics admit that God's Word is inspired. However, they do not place the same emphasis upon it. Instead they emphasize developing tradition, which they believe is just as high an authority as God's Word. Developing tradition is tradition that develops over time, meaning the Roman Catholic Church can institute new practices as time passes — and these practices must be observed by its followers.

Evangelicals do not reject certain traditions, but they believe that all traditions that are observed must adhere to the written Word of God. Traditions should not:

- Add to God's Word.
- Take away from God's Word.
- Change God's Word.
- Conflict with God's Word.

Unfortunately, many of the commanded traditions practiced by Roman Catholics are not found in Scripture and even clash with what is taught therein. The Catholic Church admittedly knows this and defends itself by saying:

- The traditions of the Church are what the Church says they are.
- Scripture means what the Church says it means.
- The people are only allowed to read the Bible in versions approved by the Catholic Church and with the help of Catholic interpretations.

Essentially, the Catholic Church is not allowing its adherents to practice the Bible freely. They almost never encourage personal Bible study, they discourage any Christian curriculums that are not Catholic, and criticize any other interpretation other than the priesthood's. This is why Catholics can tell you much about what the priest has told them, what the pope has said, what their Catechism says, but at the same time are usually illiterate when it comes to *the* highest authority of all — the Bible.

The Catholic Church assumes that people cannot understand the Bible if they are not priests, therefore, Catholic followers don't read a book they have been told they can't understand. How unfortunate. God's Word was written so that all could receive it and understand it: from the homeless to royalty. In fact, the original manuscripts of the Bible were written in *Koine* Greek. This was the common person's language of the day: basically, street language. This means God wanted everyone to read and understand his Word — not just an elite hierarchy that dictates it to everyone else.

When another authority is placed alongside the Word of God (in this case, tradition), the Word of God usually takes a backseat. Scriptural practices usually fade away and what is left are the practices of men. This is true of Catholicism. If Catholics would only open the Scripture for themselves, they would see:

- The Bible is simple to understand.
- The Bible is a source of daily spiritual life and nourishment.
- Many of the Catholic practices are nowhere taught in the Bible.

We should make God's Word the highest authority in our own lives, and this begins by reading it daily, for ourselves:

> *I have hidden your word in my heart, that I might not sin against you.*
> —*PSALM 119:11*

> *Yes, I have more insight than my teachers, for I am always thinking of your laws.*
> —*PSALM 119:99*

Question 22: Do I need to practice Catholic traditions?

As followers of Christ, we need always to keep in mind that salvation is by grace and through faith alone (Ephesians 2:8-9). So there are no traditions that we can practice that will get us into Heaven, either Catholic or Evangelical, including the sacraments. (The sacraments, Baptism and Communion, are acts of obedience that bring blessing and empowerment into our lives, but they do not determine our eternal salvation.)

With that said, there are many Catholic traditions instituted by Rome which make it the Church that it is today — none of which are mentioned in Scripture. Jesus didn't teach them, and the apostles and early Christians didn't practice them. Therefore, today's Catholic Church and the Early Christian Church are completely different from each other. This is obvious by looking at these Catholic traditions and when they were introduced. Here is a minor list[5]:

---

5 Loraine Boettner. *Roman Catholicism.* (Philadelphia, PA: The Presbyterian and Reformed Publishing Company, 1974), 7-9.

Prayers for the dead . . . . .300 AD
Veneration of angels, dead saints, and use of images . . . . .375 AD
The Mass . . . . .394 AD
Purgatory . . . . .593 AD
Praying to Mary . . . . .600 AD
Fasting on Fridays and during Lent . . . . .998 AD
Celibacy of priests . . . . .1079 AD
Selling indulgences . . . . .1190 AD
The Rosary . . . . .1090 AD
Transubstantiation (communion turns into the literal body and blood of Jesus) . . .1215 AD
Bible forbidden to be used by the common people . . . . .1229 AD
Apocryphal books added to the Bible . . . . .1546 AD
Immaculate Conception of Mary . . . . .1854 AD
Infallibility of the Pope . . . . .1870 AD
Assumption of Mary . . . . .1950 AD

Not only are these an addition to Scripture, these Catholic traditions have complicated the simplicity of the Gospel and have made following Jesus too complex. Jesus and his apostles never meant for it to be this way. Paul was constantly on guard, warning about teachers who would come into his churches while he was away and add difficult demands to the Gospel, making it into a religion of bondage instead of a message of liberty. Look what he said:

> *But I fear, lest by any means, as the serpent beguiled Eve through his subtilty,*
> *so your minds should be corrupted from the simplicity that is in Christ.*
> *—2 CORINTHIANS 11:3*

If Jesus, his apostles, and early Christians never followed the burdensome Catholic traditions, how can we be expected to follow them? If God really wanted us to follow them, he would have instructed us from his Word. But he didn't. So, if their relationship with God was complete without them, so is ours.

Today, it remains the same as Jesus taught us before Rome stepped in with its excessive demands: following Christ is as easy as following his Word. Jesus said:

> *Take my yoke upon you. Let me teach you, because I am humble*
> *and gentle at heart, and you will find rest for your souls. For my*
> *yoke is easy to bear, and the burden I give you is light.*
> *—MATTHEW 11:29-30*

How different are the words of Jesus from a list of heavy rituals. How simple the words of Christ compared to the Council of Trent (1545-1563), which proclaimed curses on those who do not practice its man-made traditions. When Jesus broke us free from oppressive religion, he warned about man-made traditions. He said:

> *For you ignore God's law and substitute your own tradition. Then he said, "You skillfully sidestep God's law in order to hold on to your own tradition. And so you cancel the word of God in order to hand down your own tradition. And this is only one example among many others.*
> —MARK 7:8,9,13

Paul said something of similar effect:

> *Don't let anyone capture you with empty philosophies and high-sounding nonsense that come from human thinking and from the spiritual powers of this world, rather than from Christ.*
> —COLOSSIANS 2:8

Serious consequences come from allowing an elite hierarchy of religious leaders to strip the common man of Scripture and, in turn, dictate unbiblical traditions in its place. Some of these consequences are:

- Sincere and devout people are misled.
- Sincere and devout people are kept from drawing closer to the Lord.
- Many zealous works are done in vain, having no eternal reward.

Instead of oppressive tradition, Jesus gave us grace and truth (John 1:17). Following the truth of Christ and receiving his grace is enough to have a deep and empowering relationship with the Lord, without all the Catholic traditions and practices. Christ said so himself:

> *And you will know the truth, and the truth will set you free.*
> —JOHN 8:32

Questions 23: Will I go to Hell if I stop practicing Catholicism?

No, absolutely not. The Catholic Church may tell you this, but the Bible does not. Those who go to Hell are there because they have rejected Jesus, not because they have left the Roman Catholic Church (John 3:16-17). Nowhere does the Bible include leaving the Roman Catholic Church as one of the sins people are suffering for in Hell (Revelation 21:8).

To further understand why leaving the Catholic Church will not condemn you to Hell, it's important to understand what the true Church is. The Bible says that the true Church was founded by Jesus Christ and is made up of all those who have received his grace through faith and have been born again:

*God has put all things under the authority of Christ and has made him head
over all things for the benefit of the church. And the church is his body; it is
made full and complete by Christ, who fills all things everywhere with himself.*
—*EPHESIANS 1:22-23*

Those who have experienced this are found in *local churches*. Local churches are groups of Christians who gather together for worship and evangelism. There were over 30 local churches seen throughout Scripture, such as Ephesus (Acts 18:19), Antioch (Acts 11:26), Corinth (Acts 18:1), and Crete (Titus 1:5). Back then, these local churches made up the one Church of Jesus Christ. The same is true today: all of those born again believers found in the myriad of local churches around the world today are united as the Church of Jesus Christ.

Because portions of God's Word are interpreted differently, denominations have sprung up within the different local churches worldwide. This doesn't mean that these denominations are divided. The subjects in Scripture that they interpret differently are not matters that change the Gospel. And though these denominations exist, there is a lot of unity among them. Here is why:

- None of these denominations claim to be the one true Church over the others.
- Each denomination recognizes the other denominations as part of the Church of Jesus Christ.
- They all agree on the essentials of the faith.
- They believe the Bible, alone, is the Word of God and the authority over their affairs.
- They are non-competitive and cooperative with one another.

The various denominations lovingly disagree and accept each other for these differences. On the other hand, the Catholic Church claims to be the only true church. As a result, it insinuates that anyone who does not adhere to its practices is not part of the true Church of Christ. In fact, the name *Catholic* means *universal*. They have felt so strongly that their traditions and practices are the true way that they have called themselves the *Catholic* Church, indicating that other denominations and sects of Christianity are not part of the Church. (Who gave them the right to assert this, anyway? Certainly not Christ.) Hence, you can see why a Roman Catholic might believe that leaving the Roman Catholic Church and quitting its practices would lead to Hell — they have been taught wrongly that Roman Catholicism is the only true Church. Leaving it leads to damnation.

But this could not be the truth: all those who have received Jesus Christ as Lord and Savior are part of the Church (Romans 10:9-10, 13). This means that the universal *catholic* church is not limited to Roman Catholicism, but includes all denominations and sects of Christianity where God's plan of salvation by grace through faith is fully embraced. The true *catholic universal Church* are those converted individuals who are serving Christ with all of their hearts, soul, mind, and strength within the various local churches and denominations around the world (Matthew 22:37).

Jesus prayed that his Church would be unified:

> *I pray that they will all be one, just as you and I are one—*
> *as you are in me, Father, and I am in you. And may they*
> *be in us so that the world will believe you sent me.*
> *—JOHN 17:21*

However, this does not mean that all Christians must mechanically fit into one denomination and become one sect, as the Roman Catholic Church teaches. It has used this Scripture for years, claiming that Evangelicals are not part of the true Church until they become Roman Catholic. But the unity that Jesus referred to here was not external and organizational. He was referring to a spiritual unity — a unity that unites local churches and denominations all around the world as brothers and sisters in the family of God. Surely, being part of God's family is much more than a few differences in interpretation, isn't it? This being the case, leaving the Roman Catholic Church and its practices is not enough to keep you out of the *true, universal, catholic Church* — God's family.

Question 24: What should I believe about Mary?

As with everything, we should believe what the Bible says about Mary and not add anything to it or take anything away from it. Maybe surprisingly to some, the Bible says very little about Mary. Here's what we know: Mary is mentioned in the genealogy of Christ (Matthew 1:16), Gabriel appears to her and announces the birth of Christ (Luke 1:26-38), she visits her cousin, Elizabeth (Luke 1:39-56), the Lord speaks to Joseph in a dream through an angel and tells him that Mary is pregnant with Jesus (Matthew 1:18-25), Mary gives birth to Jesus in Bethlehem (Matthew 2; Luke 2), Mary presents Jesus to the Lord (Luke 2:22-39), Joseph and Mary take Jesus and flee to Egypt (Matthew 2:13-21), Mary is at the wedding where Jesus performs his first miracle (John 2:1-12), she and her other sons (Jesus's brothers) come to speak with Jesus (Matthew 12:46-50), Jesus is called Mary's son (John 6:42), she is at the crucifixion of Jesus (John 19:25-27), she is present in the Upper Room when the Holy Spirit is poured out (Acts 1:14), and Paul says that Mary is the mother of Jesus (Galatians 4:4). Considering *all* that takes place in the New Testament, this is not a lot.

Outside of the birth story, Mary hardly plays a role in the New Testament. She appears only once after the public ministry of Jesus begins and disappears after the outpouring of the Spirit on Pentecost. Considering that the book of Acts covers over 30 years of Church history and Mary is not mentioned, that says her role in the foundation of the New Testament Church was minimal — definitely nowhere near what Roman Catholicism makes it today. In fact, nowhere is there any special veneration shown to Mary.

The Scripture teaches that Mary is blessed *among* women (Luke 1:42), not blessed *above* women. This simply means that Mary was God's vessel to bring the Messiah into the world. But she is just that, a vessel and not the object of our veneration. Certainly, she was a woman of great faith and virtue. She deserves our admiration, but she is not to be deified or worshiped. The Bible says that there is only one name worthy of worship, only one name that can bring salvation to those that call upon it: the name of Jesus. Notice:

> *There is salvation in no one else! God has given no other*
> *name under heaven by which we must be saved.*
> *—ACTS 4:12*

> *Therefore, God elevated him to the place of highest honor and gave him*
> *the name above all other names, that at the name of Jesus every knee*
> *should bow, in heaven and on earth and under the earth, and every*
> *tongue declare that Jesus Christ is Lord, to the glory of God the Father.*
> *—PHILIPPIANS 2:9-11*

In fact, Jesus discouraged the worship of Mary. On one occasion, a woman in the crowd raised her voice to worship Mary as Jesus walked by. She said:

> *Blessed is the womb that bare thee, and the paps which thou hast sucked.*
> *—LUKE 11:27*

Jesus didn't allow this. He replied:

> *Yea rather, blessed are they that hear the word of God, and keep it.*
> *—LUKE 11:28*

Christ made it clear that nobody else has any part in the role of salvation other than God alone. Mary was a handmaiden of the Lord, not a deity. Therefore, Mary cannot do things that only deity can do, such as to hear the prayers of billions of people and to answer them. She is not all-powerful, all-knowing, and everywhere present — as is God. God alone answers prayer. He never intended for us to treat Mary as the mediator between us and him, as Roman Catholicism usually teaches. The Bible tells us that Jesus is the mediator between God and man. In other words, it is because of Jesus (not Mary) that we can approach God without fear and ask requests of him. Notice:

> *For there is one God, and one mediator between*
> *God and men, the man Christ Jesus*
> *—1 TIMOTHY 2:5*

> *Jesus told him, "I am the way, the truth, and the life. No*
> *one can come to the Father except through me.*
> *—JOHN 14:6*

The entire Bible keeps our faith's focus on Jesus. It is through the work of Christ that we can have a deep and empowering relationship with the Lord. He, alone, is good enough and is all we need:

> *But now you have been united with Christ Jesus. Once you were far away from God, but now you have been brought near to him through the blood of Christ. For Christ himself has brought peace to us. He united Jews and Gentiles into one people when, in his own body on the cross, he broke down the wall of hostility that separated us.*
> —*EPHESIANS 2:13-14*

Question 25: What's the difference between the Catholic Bible and the Evangelical Bible?

Holding a Catholic Bible beside an Evangelical Bible, you will notice that they are pretty much the same, except an additional 15 books in the Catholic Bible. These 15 books are known as the *Apocrypha*, which means *mysterious, unknown in origin,* and *forged.* These books are *the First Book of Esdras, the Second Book of Esdras, Tobit, Judith, additions to the book of Esther, the Wisdom of Solomon, Ecclesiasticus, Baruch, the Letter of Jeremiah, the Prayer of Azariah and the Song of the Three Young Men, Susanna, Bell and the Dragon, the Prayer of Manasseh, the First Book of Maccabees, and the Second Book of Maccabees.* They are called *Apocrypha* because their validity as inspired has always been in question. Here is why:

- They were not originally written in Hebrew like the other Old Testament books.
- Around 90 AD, the Jews officially said these books should not be part of the Old Testament; they never accepted them.
- None of the writers of these books claimed inspiration.
- Christ and the apostles never quoted or made reference to these books.
- The Early Church Fathers recognized their historical value but were careful not to develop any theology from them.

For these reasons, Evangelicals have rejected them from the canon of Scripture.

While they are interesting and useful for understanding the history of Judaism, they contain doctrines that are unscriptural. They are not bad to read nor a waste of time — they are good sources of history — so long as they are not used to shape doctrines and practices.

CHAPTER 5

Isn't the Bible Too Confusing to Understand?

The Bible is the greatest book in the history of mankind. No book has been printed more, according to the Guinness World Records. Over five billion copies have been distributed around the world. But despite its record-setting popularity, there are still many people who shy away from reading it because they say they are unable to understand it; they feel intimidated or unqualified to pick it up. But the Bible is not as hard of a book as one might think — just as long as we clear up a few misunderstandings and know some basic instructions for approaching it. Then God's Word can become the greatest blessing in our lives.

Question 26: Why don't I understand the Bible?

There are a few reasons why people sense that a great gulf of difficulty lies between the Bible and their understanding:

- The Bible is a big book: There are 66 separate books in the Bible and the most popular version, the KJV, has 783,137 words. That's not exactly an *easy* read!
- The Bible doesn't have to be read chronologically: Because there are 66 separate books, readers aren't usually sure where to begin reading. Genesis? Matthew? Revelation? You can really start reading the Bible anywhere.
- There are different versions of the Bible: If you go into a bookstore, you will notice several different versions of the Bible. This isn't a bad thing, though. These versions don't differ from one another. Because the Bible was translated from Hebrew and Greek into other languages, the different versions aid each other. Different versions are also necessary because the language of the common people changes over time. As the language changes, the Bible adapts itself to the language while still holding to the original Hebrew and Greek. Reading different versions of the Bible alongside each other is fun and exciting.
- Thousands of years of history separate the Bible and us: There are customs, idioms, traditions, cultures, and manners of living in the Bible that we simply don't understand because we didn't live back then. (For example, when King Saul "went in to

cover his feet" (1 Samuel 24:3), it doesn't mean he went to put socks on. It means he looked for a place to defecate! Who would have grasped that today?)

- There are different genres in the Bible: The Bible isn't simply a narrative. Prophecy, poetry, riddles, history, songs, and letters keep the Bible from being a narrative that can be read directly from A to Z.
- The Bible is set in context: So much surrounds what is happening in the Bible that it is hard to capture the meaning of Scripture until we become familiar with the context it is set in.

Beyond the makeup of the Bible, there are several other reasons for not understanding it:

- Failure to study it: The Bible requires diligent study (2 Timothy 2:15).
- False doctrines and poor teaching: Some have been taught wrongly about Scripture by poor teachers, religious leaders, family, friends, and others. Following the blind leads to being lost (Matthew 15:9, 14).
- Closed hearts and minds: Despite the conviction of the Holy Spirit, people close their hearts and minds to God's Word because they don't like what it says (2 Timothy 4:3-4).

Question 27: Does the Bible mean different things to different people?

Over and over again it has been said, *The Bible is supposed to mean different things to different people.* This belief comes from some peculiar idea that the Bible is mystical beyond the understanding of ordinary people. While it *is* full of the supernatural works of God, the Bible is plain and clear and contains the same message for everyone who reads it. If the Bible seems to mean different things to different people, it is only because those people are reading into Scripture what they think or want it to mean instead of searching to find out what *God* meant.

The requirement for finding out what God intended the Bible to mean is to lay aside any fixed ideas and self-seeking hopes about what it should mean, and to study it thoroughly until we discover what it was written to mean. Then, when we have discovered this, we have discovered something to order our lives by that will bring God's peace and blessing.

Jesus taught us that hearing and doing his Word brings blessing, but hearing and not doing his word brings disastrous results. Notice:

> *Anyone who listens to my teaching and follows it is wise, like a person who builds*
> *a house on solid rock. Though the rain comes in torrents and the floodwaters*
> *rise and the winds beat against that house, it won't collapse because it is built*
> *on bedrock. But anyone who hears my teaching and doesn't obey it is foolish,*
> *like a person who builds a house on sand. When the rains and floods come*
> *and the winds beat against that house, it will collapse with a mighty crash.*
> *—MATTHEW 7:24-27*

Certainly he isn't talking about a different word for different people. How could what he said be possible if his word meant something different to everyone who heard it? Actually, one of the ways that people excuse themselves from doing what Jesus taught is to convince themselves it means something other than what God said it meant. Don't get caught in that trap. Just humble yourself, receive what God has to say, and adjust your life to it. This is what pleases God, and this is the correct way to approach his Word.

Question 28: I thought only special people can understand the Bible, like priests and pastors?

Some teach that only special individuals can read and understand God's Word, like priests and pastors. This discourages others from reading and studying the Bible. But God intended for all of us to handle his word. Anyone can pick up the Bible and begin studying it for understanding. Think about it:

- God commands everyone to understand his Word: How could God expect this of us if we aren't capable (Mark 7:14; Ephesians 5:17)?
- The Bible was written by common individuals: Peter was a fisherman, Luke was a doctor, Joshua was a soldier, Matthew was a tax collector, Amos was a herdsman, Paul was a rabbi, and David was a king. The Bible is for the upper class, middle class, and lower class.
- The New Testament was written in common language: During the time the New Testament was written, there were two kinds of spoken Greek: Attic Greek and Koine Greek. Attic was the language of the educated; Koine was, you might say, the street lingo. And, interestingly enough, the New Testament was written in Koine Greek. This couldn't mean anything other than that God wanted the average person to understand his Word.
- The Bible was given so people can know whether or not they are being told the truth: Without the Bible, how do we know whether a pastor or a priest is teaching the Word of God or just what they think? We have the right to look in the Word of God and search to see if what the preacher is telling us is true (Acts 17:11).

No matter who you are, God's Word if for you!

> *Yes, I have more insight than my teachers, for I am always thinking of your laws.*
> —PSALM 119:99

Question 29: Should I read the Bible or should I study the Bible?

Both! Each will help you grow in the Lord in a different way. The Bible is like milk *and* meat. Some parts of it are easy to digest and other parts of it take time and more chewing:

For when for the time ye ought to be teachers, ye have need that one
teach you again which be the first principles of the oracles of God; and
are become such as have need of milk, and not of strong meat.
—HEBREWS 5:12

Reading the Bible is like drinking milk: you move through it quickly and it goes down smoothly. When you read the Bible, you are approaching it broadly and familiarizing yourself with the stories, Scriptures, and characters. Though you will pass over things that you don't quite understand, your mind and spirit will still be refreshed. You should read the Bible every morning before starting your day. Start with a chapter or two. Your day will be dramatically different. Just as breakfast is natural fuel that gives you natural energy, God's word is spiritual fuel that will give you spiritual energy.

Whereas reading the Bible is a broad approach, studying the Bible is a concentrated approach. It is slowing down to focus on a single topic, character, verse, or story. This takes longer than just reading it so you should designate blocks of uninterrupted time for doing this. It certainly does take discipline; however, the rewards of it are tremendous. God's Word will become deeply rooted within your heart. You will become proficient at articulating and teaching the Scripture; you will be able to *divide* God's Word. Dividing God's Word means dissecting it with precision. Notice:

Study to shew thyself approved unto God, a workman that needeth
not to be ashamed, rightly dividing the word of truth.
—2 TIMOTHY 2:15

Think of a master surgeon: they understand medicine and can operate successfully without making a mess. Had they not studied, they would end up killing their patient. Teaching God's Word is no different. God wants us to teach those he places along our path. If we have done our due diligence to study, what we teach will be a blessing to these lives instead of a mess of confusion.

Question 30: How should I study the Bible?

Though inspired by God, the Bible was written by humans and for humans. In this sense, it is like any other book and should be approached like any other book. Here are some basic steps to doing that:

- Don't read your own ideas into Scripture, draw the Scriptures' ideas out: When we come to Scripture, we need to be concerned with discovering what the text says to us and not what we have to say about the text. By coming to Scripture with an open heart and mind, we are likely to gain from it what it intends to mean. The worst thing we can do is come to Scripture looking for it to support our own agenda. Doing this puts us at risk of twisting it to make it say what we want it to say. And, in this case, we will miss God's message to us.

- Find out what is going on: When studying the Bible, our best friend is context. Context determines meaning: it informs us of important things, like why something was said, to whom it was said, and if what was said is applicable to us in the 21ˢᵗ century. The best way to grasp the overall context is to read the text that precedes the Scripture we are studying and the text that follows. Doing this will set the verse we are examining in place for us to make observations about it and dig out shiny nuggets of truth that we can apply to our lives.

- Pay attention to figures of speech: Figures of speech are words used in a sense other than the normal, literal sense. Human language is filled with figures of speech and we use them everyday. For instance, *I went Christmas shopping and the whole world was at the mall,* or *The overdone steak tastes like the sole of my shoe.* The Bible is filled with figures of speech such as metaphor, simile, allegory, personification, anthropomorphism, metonymy, and hyperbole. Recognizing these and catching the meaning behind them can really open up the meaning behind a passage of Scripture. Here are a few examples:

–Hyperbole: An overstatement used for effect. Notice:

> *So if your eye—even your good eye—causes you to lust, gouge it out and throw it away. It is better for you to lose one part of your body than for your whole body to be thrown into hell. And if your hand—even your stronger hand—causes you to sin, cut it off and throw it away. It is better for you to lose one part of your body than for your whole body to be thrown into hell.*
> *—MATTHEW 5:29-30*

–Metaphor: A comparison between two unrelated things which share common characteristics. Notice:

> *You are the salt of the earth.*
> *—MATTHEW 5:13*

–Metonymy: Referring to something by referring to something associated with it. Notice:

> *Then went out to him Jerusalem, and all Judaea, and all the region round about Jordan, And were baptized of him in Jordan, confessing their sins.*
> *—MATTHEW 3:5-6*

–Personification: Representing something other than a human with the characteristics and behavior of a human. Notice:

The Red Sea saw them coming and hurried out of their
way! The water of the Jordan River turned away.
—PSALM 114:3

After we have learned how to approach Scripture, we are ready to study it. There are many methods of doing so. Here are a few:

- Chapter Analysis: Read a chapter through 10 times. Become so familiar with it that you could explain it to somebody without any trouble. Then go back through it and start investigating. (We will use Mark 8 as our example.)

First, identify all the different subjects you notice in just that one chapter. In Mark 8, we find subjects like compassion (v. 2), miracles (v. 8), unbelief (v. 12), healing (v. 25), the Kingdom of God (v. 37), and many others.

Next, ask questions about things that seem peculiar. For instance, you might might ask, *Why did Jesus pray for the blind man twice before he was healed* (v. 23-25)? *How come Jesus didn't want his disciples telling anyone he was the Christ* (v. 30)? *Why did Jesus call Peter, Satan* (v. 33)? You get the idea, right?

Then, investigate these questions: Look into commentaries, Bible dictionaries, and Bible software and see if you can find answers. If you do, make a note of them.

Finally, find other Scriptures elsewhere in the Bible that relate. For instance, you could look up other places where Jesus fed the multitude (Matthew 14:13-21; Mark 6:31-44), healed the blind (John 9:1-11), or rebuked the religious leaders (Matthew 23). As you are examining the related verses, you'll discover additional insight.

After you've identified your topics, asked questions and found answers, and learned what other related verses say, compile everything together to arrive at a conclusion. You may be surprised how much you've turned up!

- Character Study: Picking out a person of interest and studying everything the Bible says about that person can be one of the funnest studies to do. We love learning about people because we identify with them.

First, decide whom you want to study and make a list of all the places in Scripture they are mentioned. Read those passages five times each. Next, write down your impressions of that person.

For instance, if you are studying Judas Iscariot your list may include: *deceptive, sneaky, hypocritical, intelligent, thinks ahead, greedy, curious about Jesus.* Next, make an outline of their life in chronological order.

If you are studying the life of Paul, you would start with him killing Christians (Acts 8:1), add his conversion to Christ (Acts 9), include the significant events of his missionary journeys throughout Acts, and end with his last recorded words before he was martyred (2 Timothy 4).

After, look at your chronology and note the different changes and personal transformations that take place in their life. Are they growing in their understanding of Christ? Maybe they have become rebellious and turn away from God.

When you have competed this, try to find out more about the person you are studying by asking questions. If you were studying Moses, you could ask questions like, *What does the name Moses mean? What do we know about his wife, Zipporah? Why didn't Moses make it to the Promised Land?*

Finally, summarize everything you have learned into one or two paragraphs and include how you can apply it to your life.

- Background Study: Because what is going on in Scripture is so important, a background study can give you tremendous insight about your topic.

First, decide what your topic is. Next, gather reference tools such as Bible encyclopedias, Greek lexicons, commentaries, Bible dictionaries, etc. (These can be found online.) Use these to gather insights into geography, history, culture, political circumstances, and any customs during the time.

For instance, if you were studying the book of Song of Songs, you could gather info on the tents of Kedar (1:5), the vineyards of En-gedi (1:14), and the tower of David (4:4) — all of which is figurative language describing Solomon's romance with his wife. Because Solomon was the king of Israel, you could look into what kind of a relationship kings had with their wives, how they met their their wives, and what was expected of the kings' wives.

Finally, after you've finished, summarize your findings and write out an application for your own life. How is this applicable for married people? What about single people? Your research should help you draw a conclusion.

Question 31: Aren't there a whole bunch of mistakes in the Bible because men wrote it?

No, the Bible is inerrant. This means that it is incapable of being wrong. The Bible admits this:

> *The words of the Lord are pure words: as silver tried*
> *in a furnace of earth, purified seven times.*
> *—PSALM 12:6*

> *Every word of God is pure: he is a shield unto them that put their trust in him.*
> *—PROVERBS 30:5*

> *Heaven and earth shall pass away, but my words shall not pass away.*
> *—MATTHEW 24:35*

Contrary to higher liberal criticisms, there is nothing in the Word of God that contradicts science or history. The Bible does not teach inaccurate things such as the earth being created 6,000 years ago, or that the sun revolves around the earth. Those that teach this and things like it have misunderstandings and interpret the Scripture incorrectly. God's Word declares that we can trust every detail of Scripture:

> *Believing all things which are written in the law and in the prophets.*
> —*Acts 24:14b*

This means that we can trust the scientific and historical details of God's Word, without being worried the authors were too primal to understand today's advances in science or that they got their history wrong. No, the Bible was *God-breathed*, inspired revelation from Heaven. Notice:

> *All Scripture is God-breathed and is useful for teaching, rebuking,*
> *correcting and training in righteousness, so that the servant of*
> *God may be thoroughly equipped for every good work.*
> —*2 Timothy 3:16-17*

Since God always tells the truth when he speaks, we can be certain that every single detail of Scripture is true, accurate, and trustworthy. Though there will always be critics who say they have found fault, we can take comfort knowing that every criticism has a good explanation. Each dilemma can be solved as long as the critics are humble enough to accept the solution.

CHAPTER 6

Why Do I Need to Pray?

God is sovereign, meaning that he is supreme in power and authority and rules the universe. This is the reason some people often wonder why they have to pray. They think, *If God can do what he wants, why do we need to ask him?*

What makes God so unique is that, despite his ultimate sovereignty, he offers his creation choices. Notice:

> *This day I call the heavens and the earth as witnesses against*
> *you that I have set before you life and death, blessings and curses.*
> *Now choose life, so that you and your children may live.*
> —*Deuteronomy 30:15*

So, God has given humanity free will and honors how they exercise it. Therefore, God works with us and through us, not independently of us. Believe it or not, prayer is an invitation to God, welcoming him to take part in our human experience.

Throughout the Scripture we see that prayer is responsible for healing nations (2 Chronicles 7:14), protection from harm (2 Corinthians 1:8-11), forgiveness of sins (1 John 1:9), supplying our daily needs (Mark 6:11), the salvation of the lost (2 Thessalonians 3:1), and many other important things. Essentially, prayer is what causes the Kingdom of God to be a reality upon the earth (Matthew 6:9-10). You can rest assured that the prosperity of God's cause is conditioned upon prayer: the more prayer, the more God's perfect will takes place.

Questions 32: What is prayer?

Prayer is communication with God. It involves coming before God's presence and having a personal encounter with him. And while this often includes making requests from God, it also includes pouring your heart out to him (Psalm 62:8). It is during this time that we seek God's will, commit to doing what God asks of us, and worship God with a heart overflowing with love:

I love the Lord because he hears my voice and my prayer for mercy.
Because he bends down to listen, I will pray as long as I have breath!
—PSALM 116:1-2

Prayer can be done personally — just you and God (Psalm 139) — and it can be done corporately — with a group of other believers (Acts 2:1-4).

Question 33: How come prayer never seems to work for me?

Failure to pray is the result of believing that prayer doesn't work or that it is not efficient enough to be depended upon. But prayer is powerful; there is nothing more effective than reaching out to God and bringing his supernatural power into a situation. Notice:

The earnest prayer of a righteous person has great
power and produces wonderful results.
—JAMES 5:16B

So when prayer is not working, it is a sure sign that we are doing something amiss (James 4:2,3):

Ye ask, and receive not, because ye ask amiss, that
ye may consume it upon your lusts.
—JAMES 4:2-3

"Amiss" means *wrongly and inappropriately*. In other words, we can pray the wrong way and not receive because of it. Here are some things that cause our prayers to be prayed inappropriately:

- Prayer is not offered in faith: Faith is wholehearted trust in God and in his Word (Hebrews 11:1). Without faith, we cannot please God (Hebrews 11:6). So we must pray in faith, believing that God hears our prayers and will answer (Mark 11:22-24).
- Praying anxiously and fearfully: God tells us not to be anxious when we pray (Philippians 4:6). He commands us not to be afraid, because he is with us (Isaiah 41:10). Fearfulness does not move God, faith does.
- Praying for something outside of God's will: We shouldn't come to God with a bunch of selfish requests, demanding him to sign our petitions with no discretion. A genuine, day-to-day relationship with God prevents us from this kind of selfishness and inspires us to ask for things that we know are part of God's perfect plan for our lives (1 John 5:14).
- Praying for our lusts to be fulfilled: Lust is an excessive desire for pleasure. All kinds of things satisfy lust, such as money, sex, relationships, fame, power, fun, and the list goes on. Lustful prayers demand hasty answers. People who pray them expect God to

answer them *right now*. But God doesn't assist us in satisfying our lusts; he will deny our prayers every time they are an attempt to fulfill our own selfish cravings.

- Refusing to do what is needed after prayer: God doesn't just give us handouts and expect nothing of us in return; we need to add sweat to our tears. This means when we get off our knees, we need to get busy and work. We are co-laborers together with God (1 Corinthians 3:9) and we need to do our fair share of the work (2 Thessalonians 3:10).
- Unforgiveness: Jesus tells us that unless we forgive others, God will not forgive us (Matthew 6:15). This sounds harsh, but it isn't when you think about what Jesus is really telling us: the forgiveness that we have embraced for our sins through Jesus Christ should be so effective in our lives that we refuse to hold onto grudges and bitterness against other people. After all, how can we possibly hold a grudge against someone when we have offended a holy God so deeply that he had to pay with the life of his Son for us to be forgiven? Until we forgive others, God is under no obligation to answer any of our requests.
- Determining how God should answer them: Human beings tend to tell God how he should answer their prayers. They give him a timetable or expect him to answer in a certain way. Instead of limiting God, the correct attitude is surrendering to God and saying like Jesus:

Not as I will, but as You will.
—MATTHEW 26:39

Question 34: How do I pray?

God is so concerned about us succeeding in prayer that his Word tells us *how* to pray (Matthew 6:5-13). You shouldn't treat prayer like you are throwing darts at a board with a blindfold on, hoping one will hit the target. You can be skilled and efficient at it, so long as you follow God's instructions. Here are some things the Bible tells us to do when we pray:

- Don't try to impress God with flowery, lofty language: Just be you when you pray. God sees through insincere words anyway. He looks at our heart (1 Samuel 16:7).
- Don't be repetitious: Using the same words over and over again indicates generic prayer. Powerful prayer comes from the heart; it is organic and authentic. Jesus told us not to fall into the trap of thinking that the more we say something, the more liable God is to hear us. God hears us from the first time we pray. It's not the abundance of our words that move him but the sincerity of our motives (Matthew 6:7).
- Speak to the Father: Jesus was always praying to the Father and told *us* to do the same.

Pray like this: Our Father in heaven, may your name be kept holy.
—MATTHEW 6:9

At that time you won't need to ask me for anything. I tell
you the truth, you will ask the Father directly, and he will
grant your request because you use my name.
—JOHN 16:23

It is a great privilege to call the supreme God of the universe our loving father. We are his sons and daughters and, when we pray to him, we gather as family (Romans 8:15).

- Use the name of Jesus: Jesus told us to pray in his name (John 16:23). This means coming to God in Christ's place and praying for the things Jesus would pray for if he were here. It is using Jesus's authority, which he gave to us (Luke 10:19; Matthew 6:11). If we are praying on Christ's behalf, we will pray for things that move the heart of God: healing for the sick, deliverance for the oppressed, salvation for the lost, as well as for our own daily needs (Luke 4:18-19). As a result, God will answer us just as wonderfully as he answered Jesus.
- Come to God boldly: Approaching God boldly does not mean being arrogant, demanding, or entitled. No, God expects our humility (James 4:6). What it does mean, however, is coming to God without fear or intimidation.

So let us come boldly to the throne of our gracious God. There we will
receive his mercy, and we will find grace to help us when we need it most.
—HEBREWS 4:14-16

Too often God's children approach him like orphans, bowl in hand, groveling for a small answer to prayer. God doesn't like to see this. He made us his children and has given us a wonderful inheritance (Ephesians 1:11). Part of that inheritance includes the right to ask of him in prayer (Matthew 7:7-8).

- Tell God your requests: Yes, God knows what we have need of before we ask him. That means that we aren't informing God of anything when we approach him with our need. Nevertheless, he told us to ask him anyway.

Don't worry about anything; instead, pray about everything. Tell
God what you need, and thank him for all he has done.
—PHILIPPIANS 4:6

By asking God to meet our needs, we are demonstrating our dependence upon him and our desire for him to be part of our lives. Don't feel guilty for asking God for things, and don't think your requests are stupid. Your requests, however small they may be, bind you to God and release his power in your life.

- Pray in faith: Your prayer depends on your faith. Do you trust God or are you full of unbelief? If you have a hard time believing that God will answer your prayer, spend time reading his Word before you pray. Hearing his Word will produce faith and you can take that faith into prayer.

> *So then faith cometh by hearing, and hearing by the word of God.*
> —ROMANS 10:17

- Be persistent, don't give up: Often answers to prayer don't come as quickly as we would like. Sometimes there is demonic resistance to our prayers (Daniel 10) and other times God's timetable is different from ours (2 Peter 3:8). No matter what the reason may be, as long as you are praying according to God's will, you can be certain you will receive an answer to prayer. Therefore, Jesus told us not to be fainthearted and give up. Pray through the difficulty and keep your request before God.

> *One day Jesus told his disciples a story to show that*
> *they should always pray and never give up.*
> —LUKE 18:1

- Be thankful: Thanking God reminds us of all that God has done and gives us confidence in his abilities. It keeps us in faith and out of fear. And above all, thankfulness is pleasing to the Lord.

> *And always be thankful.*
> —COLOSSIANS 3:15

Question 35: Should I use a Rosary?

Peter the Hermit invented the Rosary in 1090 AD, over a thousand years after the time of Christ. It is a mechanical device made up of beads, used for counting prayers. Those who pray the Rosary begin with the sign of the cross and announce the Apostles' Creed. Then they say one Our Father, three Hail Marys, a Glory Be, and sometimes the Fatima Prayer. After, come five mysteries, consisting of one Our Father, ten Hail Marys, a Glory Be, and sometimes the Fatima Prayer. The Rosary is concluded by Hailing the Holy Queen. Roman Catholics who practice the Rosary say that the purpose of the Rosary is to contemplate Jesus through the intercession of Mary. This is why it has ten times as many prayers addressed to Mary as it does God the Father. In essence, it is a ritual to Mary.

Many who use the Rosary have a sincere and genuine love for God. In fact, they are praying the Rosary because that is the best they know how to reach God — they haven't been taught anything else. Yet, their sincerity and fervency would be better directed through praying the way Scripture teaches us to pray (see question 29), instead of using the Rosary. This is because the Rosary is not God's prescription for prayer. Consider:

- The Rosary was never used by Jesus, his disciples, or the early Church: for over 1000 years, not one single follower of Christ used a Rosary to assist them in prayer. Were their prayers, then, incomplete? Of course not. Catholic priests often teach that the more Hail Marys, the more merit is stored up in heaven. How could this be fair to Christians who lived before 1090 AD, before the Rosary was invented?
- Jesus taught us not to use *vain repetition* when we pray (Matthew 6:7-8): The Bible teaches us that our focus should not be on how many times we pray a certain prayer, as though that matters to God. God is concerned with quality, not quantity. And in God's eyes, quality prayer is prayer that comes from our own hearts and in our own words.
- Praying the Rosary gives Mary a position the Bible never gives her: Hailing the Holy Queen means recognizing Mary as sinless, but the Bible never teaches this about her. Jesus said that nobody is without sin except for God (Matthew 19:16-17). In fact, Mary, herself, acknowledged she needed a Savior to save her from sin. She said about Jesus:

> *How my spirit rejoices in God my Savior!*
> —Luke 1:47

- Only God can hear and answer prayer: Mary is not divine and does not have qualities of divinity. She cannot hear the prayers of billions of people and answer them — only God can. Mary referred to herself as God's servant, not one to be worshipped.

> *Mary responded, "I am the Lord's servant.*
> —Luke 1:38A

- Jesus is our advocate and mediator and intercessor: The Rosary gives Mary a role that belongs only to Jesus. We don't need Mary to intercede for us before God — Jesus does that for us.

> *Therefore he is able, once and forever, to save those who come to God through him. He lives forever to intercede with God on their behalf.*
> —Hebrews 7:25

Question 36: Whom should I pray to?

This is a great question; people ask it all the time. They wonder, *Should I pray to God or Jesus or the Holy Spirit?* And then they wonder, *If I pray to one and I am supposed to pray to the other, will my prayer be heard?* Let's take a breather and remember that God is One. Your prayer is heard, regardless of whom you address it to.

With that said, the Bible gives us instructions about how to *best* direct our prayers. This is because the Trinity plays a unique part in every prayer we pray. And for our understanding, we should know the roles they play for the sake of praying more efficiently. When we pray we should:

- Pray to the Father: Jesus taught us to address the Father. This doesn't mean that we cannot tell Jesus how wonderful he is or worship the Holy Spirit, especially when his presence comes upon us. It doesn't mean we can't lift our hands and uplift the name of Christ nor does it mean we cannot invite the Holy Spirit to lead and guide us. We are free to uplift, worship, and exalt the Godhead anyway that we are led. Yet, Jesus told us to *address our requests* to God the Father.

    *At that time you won't need to ask me for anything. I tell you the truth, you will
    ask the Father directly, and he will grant your request because you use my name.*
    —*JOHN 16:23*

Get into the habit of calling God your Father. God loves this. He is our source, our provider, and the one who is responsible for taking care of us. Any need or request belongs to him. And when we begin our prayer by saying *Father*, we are acknowledging this to him.

- Use the name of Jesus: When we pray in the name of Jesus, we are acknowledging to the Father that we have the right to approach him because of what Jesus has done for us. We are recognizing that our relationship with God isn't the result of our own merit, but because Jesus loved us, died for us, rose for us, and intercedes for us.

    *You can ask for anything in my name, and I will do it,
    so that the Son can bring glory to the Father.*
    —*JOHN 14:13*

- Rely on the help of the Holy Spirit: We shouldn't pray in our own strength and by our own ability. We should depend upon the power of the Holy Spirit. When we welcome the Holy Spirit to be a part of our prayers, he will literally give us the words to pray before the Father and ensure that the prayers we pray are perfect.

    Pray in the Spirit at all times and on every occasion.
    —*EPHESIANS 6:18A*

    *And the Holy Spirit helps us in our weakness. For example, we
    don't know what God wants us to pray for. But the Holy Spirit
    prays for us with groanings that cannot be expressed in words.*
    —*ROMANS 8:26*

So, when you pray you are praying to the Father in the name of Jesus, through the help of the Holy Spirit.

Here is a list of those we are *not* supposed to pray to:

- The Dead (including dead saints): Those who have died are no longer involved in earthly affairs. When Christians die, they immediately enter into the presence of the Lord (2 Corinthians 5:8). Those who are wicked are taken to Hell (John 5:28-29). They cannot hear our prayers and certainly have no power to answer them. Some believe that dead Christians have more access to God than we do because they are with God in Heaven. This simply isn't true. We who are alive have direct access to God right now and are in no need of a dead person to make requests to God on our behalf.

> *So let us come boldly to the throne of our gracious God. There we will receive his mercy, and we will find grace to help us when we need it most.*
> *—HEBREWS 4:16*

- Angels: The Bible never tells us to pray to angels. Though angels are supernatural, they aren't divine and don't have the ability to answer our prayers. Angels are not our source and will not take the place of God in our lives. In fact, they reject worship from humans (Revelation 22:8-9), and they will also reject our prayers. Angels are simply God's messengers. When it comes to prayer, their only role is helping God bring our prayers to fruition.
- Idols: Idols include anything like statues, nature, the stars, animals, etc. Not only does God forbid idolatry (Exodus 20:3), idols aren't alive and don't answer prayer.

> *What good is an idol carved by man, or a cast image that deceives you?*
> *How foolish to trust in your own creation—a god that can't even talk!*
> *—HABAKKUK 2:18*

Question 37: How often should I pray?

It is always a good time to pray. God's Word tells us that we should always be in an attitude of prayer:

> *Never stop praying.*
> *—1 THESSALONIANS 5:17*

Remember, prayer is communication with God. We can communicate with God all day long: when we wake up (Psalm 63:1), when we are happy (Luke 1:47), when we are sad (Habakkuk 3:17-18), before we eat (1 Timothy 4:4-5), and even late at night (Luke 6:12).

As Christians, we should develop and maintain a prayer life. A prayer life is a daily time of personal prayer and worship to God. When we are consistent about praying every day, we will notice our relationship with God becoming more powerful, and producing wonderful results.

Question 38: What will happen to me when I pray?

We should expect to see wonderful results in our lives when we pray. The Scripture tells us this:

> *The earnest prayer of a righteous person has great*
> *power and produces wonderful results.*
> —JAMES 5:16B

We can rest assured that God's supernatural power will surround every aspect of our lives when we become serious about prayer. Here are some results we can expect to see:

- We will stay full of the Holy Spirit: When we spend daily time praying by the power of the Holy Spirit, we spend daily time experiencing God. This enables the Holy Spirit to occupy every part of our lives and control us. In other words, prayer surrenders us to the Holy Spirit so that we can quickly obey him and live fruitful lives for the Kingdom. Not only this, but prayer causes the presence of the Holy Spirit to become apparent in our lives. This means that when others are around us, they will sense that God's Spirit is with us. And as a result, we can minister to them by the Spirit's power so their lives can be transformed.

> *I pray that God, the source of hope, will fill you completely with*
> *joy and peace because you trust in him. Then you will overflow*
> *with confident hope through the power of the Holy Spirit.*
> —ROMANS 15:13

- We won't be worriers: Prayer gives us the unique privilege to hurl our cares over onto God. Stress is the result of trying to handle our problems on our own. It is senseless to do this when God has told us to give our problems to him!

> *Don't worry about anything; instead, pray about everything. Tell God*
> *what you need, and thank him for all he has done. Then you will*
> *experience God's peace, which exceeds anything we can understand. His*
> *peace will guard your hearts and minds as you live in Christ Jesus.*
> —PHILIPPIANS 4:6-7

- We will hate sin the way God hates it: God *hates* sin; it disgusts him. We experience this same loathing for sin when we spend time around him. When this happens, we develop a heart that doesn't want to disappoint God, and we keep away from sin.

Anyone who continues to live in him will not sin.
—1 John 3:6a

- We will think bigger: God shares his ideas with us in prayer. And nothing about God's ideas is small.

  I wisdom dwell with prudence, and find out knowledge of witty inventions.
  —Proverbs 8:12

- We will become bolder: Boldness is the ability to lead; it is saying and doing the right things despite opposition. In order to be bold, we must be lovers of the truth. And nothing causes our love for the truth to become white-hot like prayer.

  And now, O Lord, hear their threats, and give us, your
  servants, great boldness in preaching your word.
  —Acts 4:29

- We will understand spiritual things better: People who are not spiritual cannot understand spiritual things (1 Corinthians 2:14). When we approach the Lord and ask him for help, the Holy Spirit opens up the eyes of our understanding so that we can comprehend the things of God. This makes us spiritual.

  Asking God, the glorious Father of our Lord Jesus Christ, to give you
  spiritual wisdom and insight so that you might grow in your knowledge
  of God. I pray that your hearts will be flooded with light so that you
  can understand the confident hope he has given to those he called—
  his holy people who are his rich and glorious inheritance.
  —Ephesians 1:17-18

- God's Protection: Prayer is a powerful weapon that spoils the evil plans of Satan.

  And you are helping us by praying for us. Then many people will give thanks
  because God has graciously answered so many prayers for our safety.
  —2 Corinthians 1:11

- Miracles: Expectation is the breeding ground for miracles. Prayer causes us to expect God to do something miraculous in our lives. This faith and expectation moves the hand of God to start working mightily on our behalf.

  You are blessed because you believed that the Lord would do what he said.
  —Luke 1:45

CHAPTER 7
Church — What's the Point?

Going to church — for many, it feels like such a drag. It's that thing that comes between late-night fun on Saturday and brunch on Sunday — an inconvenient disruption to the weekend festivities. People who dread going to church think, *If I want God to be happy this week, I'll just have to wake up early, find a shirt to wear, and listen to the preacher for hopefully no more than 45 minutes, although these days, no more than 25 minutes.* The majority of people don't like going to church. It's a personal chore, like folding laundry.

But there are some people who love going to church. Up early, coffee brewing, singing a favorite spiritual, and expecting something good from God — no, not good: wonderful! They pile the kids in the car, arrive early to serve, greet people as they walk in, and raise their hands in worship — sometimes with tears trickling off their cheeks. Are they religious fanatics? Maybe they are just old school? Or maybe — just maybe — what they have experienced in church has changed their lives. After all, going to church is God's idea. It only makes sense for it to be life-changing:

> *And let us not neglect our meeting together, as some people do, but encourage*
> *one another, especially now that the day of his return is drawing near.*
> *—HEBREWS 10:25*

God didn't invent going to church to punish us and spoil our fun on the weekends. We need church; it's vital to spiritual growth and Christian victory. We come together as believers — those who've had a personal encounter with Jesus Christ — and lift up the name of the Lord. We report what God has done in our lives throughout the week and cheer one another on to victory. This is the most precious time of the week because it touches what is most important in our lives: our relationship with Jesus. If our relationship with Jesus is alive, going to church isn't just necessary, it's exciting.

Question 39: Why should I go to church?

"I don't need to go to church to get into heaven," says everyone who believes in God but doesn't go to church. Well, they are correct: eternal life is by grace through faith and not by works

(Ephesians 2:8-9). Technically, you don't ever have to step foot in a church to ensure your place in heaven. But, if God has saved you, why wouldn't you want to? What is it about being part of a church that magnifies Jesus, spreads the Gospel through evangelism and missions, and stands behind you to help you overcome temptation that is so bad? Those who make this statement miss the big point: God's call for our lives isn't just getting into heaven. While we are here on the earth, it is using our lives to glorify him. In order to do that, we need a church home and a pastor that equips us, teaches us, trains us, and if need be, corrects us until Jesus returns:

> Now these are the gifts Christ gave to the church: the apostles, the prophets, the evangelists, and the pastors and teachers. Their responsibility is to equip God's people to do his work and build up the church, the body of Christ. This will continue until we all come to such unity in our faith and knowledge of God's Son that we will be mature in the Lord, measuring up to the full and complete standard of Christ. Then we will no longer be immature like children. We won't be tossed and blown about by every wind of new teaching. We will not be influenced when people try to trick us with lies so clever they sound like the truth. Instead, we will speak the truth in love, growing in every way more and more like Christ, who is the head of his body, the church.
> —EPHESIANS 4:11-15

Beside this, going to church:

- Was practiced by the New Testament Christians: New converts immediately became church goers to grow in Christ. In fact, most of the New Testament is made up of letters written to churches full of Christians, not to individual Christians (Revelation 2-3).
- Identifies us as part of a congregation: God has given his pastors and church leaders the responsibility of overseeing us (Acts 20:28). In order for them to assume this responsibility, we must identify ourselves to them as being part of their congregation.
- Ensures us that our faith is not our own self-made religion: Loners isolate themselves because they want to practice their own version of Christianity instead of what God instructs us to practice from his Word. Being part of a local church provides us with checks and balances and helps us follow the truth accurately (Jude 3).
- Keeps us from wandering: Jesus calls us all sheep (John 10:3). Sheep need a shepherd, otherwise they wander away. Jesus is our Great Shepherd and he has assigned us to under shepherds, known as pastors (1 Peter 5:2,4). Being part of a congregation gives us the leadership of a shepherd and enables us all to follow Christ as one.

Question 40: Do I get points for going to church?

No. God does not keep track of our church attendance using the merit system. Answers to our prayers aren't based upon how many times God has seen us in church this month. God's favor toward us is the result of what Christ has done in our stead, not our remarkable church attendance:

> *So we praise God for the glorious grace he has poured*
> *out on us who belong to his dear Son.*
> —*EPHESIANS 1:6*

On the other hand, skipping church doesn't make God mad, in and of itself. We may actually have a good reason that keeps us from making it to church on a particular morning. God certainly is big enough to see past that.

God is concerned with our hearts. And he finds people with soft hearts and with hard hearts. Soft hearts desire to be molded and shaped by God's Word. They want to hear what is in God's Word in order to obey. But hard hearts aren't concerned with what God's Word has to say because they believe their way is better. Soft hearts draw near to God, and hard hearts turn away (Ezekiel 36:26; Matthew 13:14-15).

Now a person with a hard heart may come to church one morning (perhaps out of guilt) and a person with a soft heart may stay home from church one morning (perhaps they need to rest), but God knows the difference. He looks past the pew and sees the motive:

> *People judge by outward appearance, but the Lord looks at the heart.*
> —*1 SAMUEL 16:7B.*

So instead of wondering what God thinks of our church attendance, we should ask ourselves why we go to church or why we don't. This will reveal everything we truly need to be concerned with.

Question 41: Can't I just listen to preaching on YouTube instead of going to church?

Technology is wonderful. Because of the Internet, we can watch sermons and hear God's Word all day long if we want to. It's such a blessing to have God's Word so accessible. But at the same time, this should not replace going to church. Those who think so, mistakenly believe that church is *only* about hearing God's Word. While that is very important, it isn't all there is to it. Going to church also includes:

- Being with other Christians: We can't run this race alone. We need the camaraderie of our brothers and sisters in Christ (1 Thessalonians 5:11).
- Corporate prayer and worship: Corporate prayer should be one of the priorities of a Christian. We should constantly be gathering ourselves to intercede for what is taking place in our church, city, country, and world (Acts 12:12; 1 Timothy 2:2-4).

- Accountability: Christians should not be secretive, because sin is accomplished in secret. Instead, we should be happy to live our lives in front of our church leaders and Christian brothers and sisters (Philippians 1:27).
- Fellowship: One of the greatest parts about going to church is developing deep, meaningful relationships with like-minded Christians. These relationships are good for linking together in prayer and watching out for one another in this dark world full of hostility towards Christians (Acts 2:42).
- The opportunity to serve: God desires each Christian to offer their talents and abilities to their local church for the purpose of meeting the needs of believers and reaching the lost for Christ (1 Peter 4:10-11).

Question 42: Does the Church need me?

Yes. God tells us that we are all valuable to the Church. In fact, God calls the Church his Body. This metaphor is used to imply that God's people are diverse. And within the vast diversity, we each have something to add. Notice:

> *Yes, the body has many different parts, not just one part. If the foot says, "I am not a part of the body because I am not a hand," that does not make it any less a part of the body. And if the ear says, "I am not part of the body because I am not an eye," would that make it any less a part of the body? If the whole body were an eye, how would you hear? Or if your whole body were an ear, how would you smell anything? But our bodies have many parts, and God has put each part just where he wants it. How strange a body would be if it had only one part! Yes, there are many parts, but only one body. The eye can never say to the hand, "I don't need you." The head can't say to the feet, "I don't need you."*
> *—1 Corinthians 12:14-21*

When we give our lives to Christ, our abilities, talents, intelligence, and energy become his. And God uses them to meet the needs of his church. Notice:

> *In his grace, God has given us different gifts for doing certain things well.*
> *—Romans 12:6a*

So whatever your ability may be, you can use it to serve God by offering it to your local church. Perhaps you are a handy person, good at fixing things. Why not make time to lend your church a hand? Maybe you have a wonderful voice. Instead of singing to entertain the world, join the choir and sing for Jesus. Some people are great with children — they should help in the nursery and with children's church. You get the point.

When we become galvanized about using our talents for Jesus, his Body grows and we are able to reach more people for the Kingdom.

Question 43: What should I experience in church?

While it is not our job to criticize, there *are* some things that we should look for in a church when we are seeking to be part of one. Here is a list of things from Scripture that make up a church that pleases the Lord:

- The gifts of the Holy Spirit are present: The gifts of the Spirit are supernatural abilities from the Holy Spirit, useful for ministering to others (1 Corinthians 12:7-11) (see chapter 9). When these gifts are in manifestation, it is evidence that the Holy Spirit is in control of the service and that his presence is near.

- The Word of God is preached and taught: God's Word should be the only thing preached and taught during service (1 Timothy 4:13). The pulpit is not the place for politics, psychology, stand up comedy, conspiracy theories, and the myriad of other things that take people's attention away from hearing and learning God's Word.

- Salvations, healings, miracles, and deliverances are taking place: The ministry of Jesus was teaching, preaching, and healing (Matthew 9:35). He commissioned his disciples to do the same and said that signs and wonders would follow them wherever they went (Mark 16:15-18). Therefore, church should be a place where the mighty power of the Holy Spirit breaks the power of Satan (Acts 10:38).

- The leadership has character: Character is strong moral fiber. It means having integrity, making choices that please the Lord, and behaving like a Christian (Galatians 5:22-23). When ministerial leadership demonstrates upright character, the church is sure to follow.

- The church edifies, not entertains: Entertainment is holding a person's attention through amusement. Church shouldn't exist to amuse. The worship shouldn't be a concert and the preaching shouldn't be a show. Now there isn't anything wrong with having fun at church, so long as having fun doesn't take away from what people should be there for— to have an encounter with God.

- Diligence in prayer: Prayer should be the foundation of every church. This means having constant prayer meetings and even corporate fasts for the purpose of seeking God (Acts 6:4).

- Reaching the lost: God's people should be zealous about going out and finding the lost and leading them to Jesus. This means soul-winning through things such as street evangelism, missions work, and various outreaches (Luke 14:23).

- A white-hot love for Jesus: Above all, the church should be genuine and fervent about its love for Christ. This fervor should be felt in service. The atmosphere shouldn't be dry, cold, and lifeless. It should have a pulse and be powerful, dynamic, and lively — all fueled by a genuine love for Jesus and an expectation for him to return (Revelation 2:4).

- Imperfection: No church is perfect. The fact is, churches are full of imperfect people who are growing everyday in the Lord. They haven't arrived just yet, which means churches are sure to make mistakes. Be as gracious with churches as you expect others to be with you.

Ultimately, we need to pray and ask the Holy Spirit where we belong. In the end, the choice is his and not our own. Since he is the one who tells us where to go, he is the only one who can give us permission to leave. Too often people just leave their church without the decree of the Holy Spirit. Someone offends them, the pastor does something they don't like, the worship teams starts singing songs they haven't heard, and these people never come back. This is carnal behavior and it doesn't please the Lord. Ask God to bring you to the right church and, when he does, stay there until he says otherwise.

CHAPTER 8
Who Is the Holy Spirit?

The Holy Spirit tends to be a person of mystery. It's easy to understand the Father: in the Old Testament we see him at work in creation and as the Sovereign Lord of all. And then we see Jesus — the Word made flesh — living upon the earth, preaching the Kingdom, and destroying the works of Satan. Yet, it seems that we have to work overtime to place the Holy Spirit. For one, he is called a *Spirit*. In our minds, a spirit tends to portray the idea of an evasive being. He is also spoken of figuratively a lot: he descends upon Jesus like a dove (Luke 3:22), Jesus compares him to the wind (John 3:8), and his presence is described as burning fire (Acts 2:3). Needless to say, our idea of the Holy Spirit can get hung up on the symbolism. As a result, the third person of the Godhead sometimes remains ambiguous to our understanding.

But God desires for us to know all about the Holy Spirit. Before Jesus went to the cross, he spent his last evening familiarizing his disciples with him (John 14-16). Jesus told them that the Holy Spirit was soon to come and explained what he would do when he arrived. Then the Holy Spirit showed up and has been here ever since (Acts 2). Now, not only can we know all about him, we can have a personal relationship with him. This is God's desire.

Question 44: Is the Holy Spirit a person, like the Father and Son?

The first thing we must know about the Holy Spirit is that he is a person, just as much as the Father is a person and the Son is a person. So if we think that he is a force or an impersonal being, we need stop. He is never called an *it*, but always *he* (John 15:26). The Holy Spirit is intelligent (1 Corinthians 2:10), has a will (1 Corinthians 12:11), and can even he have his feelings hurt (Ephesians 4:30). So it is important to treat the Holy Spirit like a person:

- Welcome him to be a part of your day.
- Ask him for his help.
- Be aware of his presence.
- Seek to please him in everything you do.

Question 45: Does he live in me?

Absolutely. The Holy Spirit dwells inside each person who has given their life to Christ. We literally have God inside of us!

> *Don't you realize that your body is the temple of the Holy Spirit, who lives in you and was given to you by God? You do not belong to yourself, for God bought you with a high price. So you must honor God with your body.*
> *—1 CORINTHIANS 6:19-20*

In the Old Testament, before Christ died on the cross, the presence of God would appear in the Jew's temple once a year (Hebrews 9:7). After Christ, all of that changed. His presence no longer dwells in the Temple (the Temple doesn't even exist anymore), it dwells in us. And his presence dwells in us because the Holy Spirit lives in us. *We* are God's temple, *we* are his habitation:

> *He is the Holy Spirit, who leads into all truth. The world cannot receive him, because it isn't looking for him and doesn't recognize him. But you know him, because he lives with you now and later will be in you.*
> *—JOHN 14:17*

Obviously, if God lives inside of us, our lives will reflect it. Here are some things that happen as soon as the Holy Spirit moves in. These are evidences that he is there:

- Life changes: You can literally see the change in a person's eyes after the Holy Spirit has settled inside of them. There is a glow that emits joy, peace, love, and hope. It's the look of someone who has found what they've been looking for.

> *This means that anyone who belongs to Christ has become a new person. The old life is gone; a new life has begun!*
> *—2 CORINTHIANS 5:17*

- We receive confidence that we are part of God's family: We might be going about our day when — out of nowhere — we suddenly become conscious of our place in God's family. This is the Holy Spirit doing his job. He is our constant witness that we have been adopted into God's heavenly family.

> *For his Spirit joins with our spirit to affirm that we are God's children.*
> *—ROMANS 8:16*

- The Bible becomes alive: The author of the Bible now lives within. He is a constant aid to our understanding so that we can comprehend the Word and then act on it.

> *And we have received God's Spirit (not the world's spirit), so we*
> *can know the wonderful things God has freely given us.*
> *—1 CORINTHIANS 2:12*

- Our prayer life becomes powerful: The Holy Spirit always knows the perfect prayer and empowers us to pray it.

> *And the Holy Spirit helps us in our weakness. For example, we*
> *don't know what God wants us to pray for. But the Holy Spirit*
> *prays for us with groanings that cannot be expressed in words.*
> *—ROMANS 8:26*

- We long to please God: Pleasing God above ourselves becomes our greatest desire. In every situation, we stop to think how we can bring glory to the Lord. This means resisting sin, no matter the cost.

> *My old self has been crucified with Christ. It is no longer I who*
> *live, but Christ lives in me. So I live in this earthly body by trusting*
> *in the Son of God, who loved me and gave himself for me.*
> *—GALATIANS 2:20*

Question 46: What does the Holy Spirit do?

The Holy Spirit is very active and is at work in every country, city, and village in the world. Ever since he arrived, he has been relentlessly working with human beings to further his plan upon the earth. His work isn't limited to just one thing, but varies. Here is what the Bible says he does:

- Promotes Jesus: Our faith in the work of Christ brings salvation. Therefore, the Holy Spirit works through his people to promote, uplift, and bring attention to Jesus. His job is to see to it that humanity is impressed with the Lord.

> *He will bring me glory by telling you whatever he receives from me.*
> *—JOHN 16:14*

- Convicts us: It's not our job to make people sorrowful for their sin — it's the Holy Spirit's.

> *And when he comes, he will convict the world of its sin, and*
> *of God's righteousness, and of the coming judgment.*
> *—JOHN 16:8*

- Guides us: The Holy Spirit is our life's tour guide. He sees the future, he knows what is ahead, and he prompts us to make the best choices and right decisions.

> *When the Spirit of truth comes, he will guide you into all*
> *truth. He will not speak on his own but will tell you what*
> *he has heard. He will tell you about the future.*
> *—JOHN 16:13*

- Manifests his presence: The Holy Spirit is always with us because he is in us. This means he will never leave us. Yet, there are times when his presence can felt more strongly. When he manifests his presence, the atmosphere turns divine. There is an abundance of joy, peace, hope, wisdom, power, and might. This might happen when we are in prayer, in church, or even talking with a friend about the Lord in a booth at a restaurant.

> *For the Kingdom of God is not a matter of what we eat or drink, but*
> *of living a life of goodness and peace and joy in the Holy Spirit.*
> *—ROMANS 14:17*

- Works miracles, signs, and wonders: The Spirit of God is powerful and supernatural. When he works, he is not confined to the limitations of time or the laws of science. Unexplainable things occur when the presence of the Lord manifests: tumors disappear, bones straighten up, blind eyes open, deaf ears hear, and the dead can be raised.

> *And now I will send the Holy Spirit, just as my Father promised. But stay here*
> *in the city until the Holy Spirit comes and fills you with power from heaven.*
> *—LUKE 24:49*

- Empowers us: The Holy Spirit gives us a supernatural testimony of Jesus. When he empowers us, our witness won't be dry and boring. It will be convincing and alive… and powerful! Often, this testimony is backed up with miracles, healings, and deliverances — all of which prove to those listening that Jesus is Lord.

> *But you will receive power when the Holy Spirit comes upon you. And*
> *you will be my witnesses, telling people about me everywhere—in*
> *Jerusalem, throughout Judea, in Samaria, and to the ends of the earth.*
> *—ACTS 1:8*

Question 47: How do I receive the Holy Spirit's empowerment?

The empowerment of the Holy Spirit to witness about Jesus is called the Baptism in the Holy Spirit.

Baptize means to totally submerge. Normally we associate baptism with being dunked in water after confessing Jesus as Lord. Sure, this is baptism in water. But as the word itself is defined, just about anything can be baptized. A cookie can be baptized in milk, a submarine can be baptized in the ocean, and a Christian can be baptized in the Holy Spirit's life and power.

John the Baptist said that Jesus desires us to be baptized in the Spirit:

> *John answered their questions by saying, "I baptize you with water;*
> *but someone is coming soon who is greater than I am—so much greater*
> *that I'm not even worthy to be his slave and untie the straps of his*
> *sandals. He will baptize you with the Holy Spirit and with fire.*
> —*LUKE 3:16*

The Baptism in the Holy Spirit is different from the indwelling presence of the Holy Spirit that we experience at salvation, discussed in question 45. The indwelling presence of the Holy Spirit is for *us* — it is God living in us. The Baptism in the Holy Spirit is for *others* — it comes upon us and empowers us to minister.

The indwelling of the Holy Spirit is available for sinners to receive; the Baptism in the Holy Spirit is only available to those who are saved. That's not to say that it's impossible for someone to get saved and then receive the Baptism in the Spirit a second later. That happens often!

The way we receive the Spirit's empowerment is through:

- Seeking God: God responds to our hunger and desire. Desire gives us access to the blessings of God. Apathy restricts our access to what God has for us because God never forces us to take anything we don't want.

> *Keep on asking, and you will receive what you ask for. Keep on*
> *seeking, and you will find. Keep on knocking, and the door will be*
> *opened to you. For everyone who asks, receives. Everyone who seeks,*
> *finds. And to everyone who knocks, the door will be opened.*
> —*MATTHEW 7:7-8*

- Being bold to ask: Some people fear that if they ask God for the Baptism in the Spirit, God might give them something they don't want instead. We must trust that God will give us exactly what we ask for if what we are requesting is in line with his will. And certainly, the Baptism in the Holy Spirit is his will.

> *"You fathers—if your children ask[e] for a fish, do you give them a snake*
> *instead? Or if they ask for an egg, do you give them a scorpion? Of course not!*
> *So if you sinful people know how to give good gifts to your children, how much*
> *more will your heavenly Father give the Holy Spirit to those who ask him.*
> —*LUKE 11:11-13*

- Believe that you will receive: Faith is believing that God will give us what we ask for. Our faith grows the more that we hear God's Word (Romans 10:17; Galatians 3:2). If you are having trouble believing that you will receive the Baptism in the Holy Spirit, you can take more time to learn about it so that your faith can grow to a place where you can receive it.

> *You can pray for anything, and if you have faith, you will receive it.*
> —MATTHEW 21:22

Question 48: What happens when I receive the Baptism in the Holy Spirit?

After we receive the Baptism in the Holy Spirit, a notable change will immediately take place in our lives. We will go *from glory to glory* in our relationship with the Lord (2 Corinthians 3:18). In other words, we'll take on a new dimension of power and authority. Here is why:

- We receive new power to witness: Once we get it, telling people about Jesus becomes very important. Not only that, but our witness becomes convincing — people will be moved by what we're saying!

> *And now, O Lord, hear their threats, and give us, your servants, great boldness in preaching your word. Stretch out your hand with healing power; may miraculous signs and wonders be done through the name of your holy servant Jesus. After this prayer, the meeting place shook, and they were all filled with the Holy Spirit. Then they preached the word of God with boldness.*
> —ACTS 4:29-31

- We receive the ability to speak in tongues: Speaking in tongues accompanies the Baptism in the Holy Spirit. This is a prayer language that we can use privately to communicate with God. When we pray in tongues, we are praying the perfect will of God. As a result, we are edified and built up.

> *And everyone present was filled with the Holy Spirit and began speaking in other languages, as the Holy Spirit gave them this ability.*
> -ACTS 2:4

> *For if you have the ability to speak in tongues, you will be talking only to God, since people won't be able to understand you. You will be speaking by the power of the Spirit, but it will all be mysterious.*
> -1 CORINTHIANS 14:2

- We become sensitive to the Holy Spirit: Praying in tongues causes our spirits to become more sensitive to the leading of the Holy Spirit. The more time we spend fellowshipping with him, the easier it is to recognize him at work.

> *For, "Who can know the Lord's thoughts? Who knows enough to teach him?" But we understand these things, for we have the mind of Christ.*
>
> *-1 CORINTHIANS 2:16*

- The gifts of the Spirit become more active in our lives: The closer we are to the Holy Spirit, the more the gifts of the Spirit become active in our lives because the Holy Spirit is their source. It is more common to see the genuine manifestation of the gifts of the Spirit in a church that preaches the Baptism in the Holy Spirit than in a church that doesn't.

> *It is the one and only Spirit who distributes all these gifts. He alone decides which gift each person should have.*
>
> *-1 CORINTHIANS 12:11*

CHAPTER 9

Do Christians Have Super Powers?

God has given us the privilege of working together with him to minister to those who are hurting and in need (2 Corinthians 5:19-21). Some of these needs are so deep that our own human ability just isn't enough to suffice. This is where God's supernatural power takes over. And supernatural things always happen when God helps his people.

The Bible is chock-full of natural people doing supernatural things when God's Spirit comes upon them. Peter and John were fishermen, but they were used to heal a crippled beggar. Elijah was just as human as we are, but he outran a chariot (which normally goes 35-40 mph). Daniel was thrown into a den of hungry lions, but wasn't eaten. And, though men wrote the Bible, over 2,000 prophecies have come to pass without any errors. These are just a *few* of the mighty works that the Spirit of God has done through those who have walked with him.

Today, miracles continue to take place all over the world. Christians in every country will tell you that they have watched the sick get healed, the lame walk, and the blind see. Miracles of supernatural provision, divine visitations, and unexplainable signs that point to Jesus as Lord are quite common — not rare.

It's not that Christians have super powers in and of themselves. Rather, it is the Spirit of God working mightily in us and through us; it is assistance from the Kingdom of God. The Holy Spirit makes it known to us that he is here. And this he does through what the Bible calls the gifts of the Spirit.

Question 49: What are the gifts of the Spirit?

The gifts of the Spirit are special abilities that the Holy Spirit gives us to do the work of the Kingdom and minister to others.

> *For to one is given by the Spirit the word of wisdom; to another the word*
> *of knowledge by the same Spirit; To another faith by the same Spirit; to*
> *another the gifts of healing by the same Spirit; To another the working of*

miracles; to another prophecy; to another discerning of spirits; to another divers kinds of tongues; to another the interpretation of tongues.
-*1 CORINTHIANS 12:8-10*

Nine are listed. They are:

- Word of Wisdom: This is supernatural wisdom concerning a matter or circumstance that we can't figure out on our own. It's revelation concerning God's will. It can come as a solution to a problem, an idea, a course of action, and even counsel (Genesis 41:33-36).

- Word of Knowledge: This is supernatural knowledge about something that we couldn't know on our own. It can be about a person, place, thing, situation, or spiritual matter. It exposes, warns, or informs (Acts 9:10-12).

- Faith: This is the gift of faith — special faith — as some say, not to be confused with saving faith in Christ. Special faith enables us to fulfill a distinct assignment that God has given. It trusts God — no matter how crazy the circumstances might look — expecting miracles and receiving miracles (Daniel 6:23).

- Gifts of Healing: This is healing of all the various sicknesses and diseases without any natural help (Acts 10:38).

- Working of Miracles: Though all the gifts of the Spirit are miraculous, the working of miracles refers to specific acts that supersede the laws of nature and time, and suspend the natural order (Matthew 14:13-21).

- Prophecy: This is speaking under the inspiration of the Holy Spirit. Prophecy means *to flow forth* and *to speak to one another*. So when we prophesy, a supernatural message flows from our lips and encourages, uplifts, and teaches others (1 Corinthians 14:3).

- Discerning of Spirits: It's the tendency for some to call this the *gift of discernment* and assume it means discerning people's faults and failures. But that's incorrect. This is the discerning of *spirits*, meaning supernatural insight into the spirit realm. It includes discerning the presence of evil spirits, seeing the similitude of Christ, and perceiving what kind of spirit is working through another person (Isaiah 6:1).

- Tongues: This is supernatural utterance in a language that has not been learned — be it a heavenly language or human language (1 Corinthians 13:1). It can be used in private for personal prayer and it can be used in public to address those who are present. When used to give a message in public, it requires an interpretation (1 Corinthians 14:2).

- Interpretation of Tongues: This is interpreting an unknown tongue, supernaturally. It can be done privately during personal prayer and it can be done publically, after a message in an unknown tongue is given (1 Corinthians 14:5).

These nine gifts can be broken up into three categories:

- The Revelation Gifts (they reveal something): Word of wisdom, word of knowledge, and discerning of spirits.
- The Power Gifts (they do something): Special faith, gifts of healing, and working of miracles.
- The Utterance Gifts (they communicate something): Prophecy, tongues, and interpretation of tongues.

Question 50: Do I have any gifts of the Spirit?

We can be certain that God desires the gifts of the Spirit to work in each of our lives. *But which one,* you might ask? It depends. The Holy Spirit distributes these gifts based upon the task that God has given us:

> *There are different kinds of spiritual gifts, but the same Spirit is the source of them all. It is the one and only Spirit who distributes all these gifts. He alone decides which gift each person should have.*
> *-1 CORINTHIANS 7:7,11*

We can be certain that if we seek God, walk closely with the Holy Spirit, and obey what he tells us to do, the gifts of the Spirit will start showing up in our lives. You may start seeing God use you to minister healing to the sick or God may give you a word of knowledge for someone. It's all very exciting.

When this begins to happen, remember that God is supplying these gifts based upon what he has called you to do. They are tools for your service to the Lord. Don't limit yourself to just one gift — believe that they will all show up in your life. God has called you to do great things; you'll need all the tools you can get!

Question 51: What if I am not good enough for the gifts of the Spirit?

If receiving the gifts of the Spirit were based upon how good we are, none of us would qualify as recipients. We've all sinned and come short of God's standard (Romans 3:23). But God has extended us his grace, and that includes the gifts of the Spirit (Ephesians 2:8-9). The past is no longer a factor when it comes to the gifts of the Spirit.

If we live obediently, we can be confident that the gifts of the Spirit will be a normal part of our lives. Living obediently includes refraining from sin, resisting temptation, and following the promptings of the Spirit. It also includes seeking God through prayer, reading his Word, and setting ourselves apart from worldliness. God works through vessels that are reserved for his holy use:

> *Because we have these promises, dear friends, let us cleanse ourselves from everything that can defile our body or spirit. And let us work toward complete holiness because we fear God.*
> *-2 CORINTHIANS 7:1*

Question 52: How do I receive the gifts of the Spirit?

We receive the gifts of the Spirit by seeking them with passion:

> *So you should earnestly desire the most helpful gifts.*
> —*1 Corinthians 12:31*

As we seek God, we will become concerned with the things *he* is concerned about. Our hearts may start breaking for sick people or we may begin to agonize over the lost. It's even possible that God will place a special burden in our heart that requires a miracle in order to take place. When this happens God will give us the supernatural tools to get the job done.

Ask! Tell him you need his gifts! Let him know you are available and desire to be used! Then get ready...

Question 53: Which gift is the best?

The gifts of the Spirit are all supernatural and divine — there is no hierarchy of gifts, one is not better than the other. Remember, they are tools. The best tool is the tool needed to complete a job. Think of a butter knife and a chainsaw: which is better? It depends on the task. If cutting down a tree is the task, the chainsaw is better. If cutting a sandwich is the task, obviously the knife. So if someone needs healing, the gifts of healing are best. If a problem needs to be solved, it's the word of wisdom. God always meets the need; he always supplies the right tool — the best tool.

Our concern should be with using our tools the correct way, out of love:

> *If I could speak all the languages of earth and of angels, but didn't love others,*
> *I would only be a noisy gong or a clanging cymbal. If I had the gift of prophecy,*
> *and if I understood all of God's secret plans and possessed all knowledge, and if*
> *I had such faith that I could move mountains, but didn't love others, I would*
> *be nothing. If I gave everything I have to the poor and even sacrificed my body,*
> *I could boast about it; but if I didn't love others, I would have gained nothing.*
> *-1 Corinthians 13:1-3*

The gifts are not to bring attention to ourselves, generate a following, or bolster our ego. They are to care for God's people the same way he would care for them if he were here in a body.

CHAPTER 10

Does God Need Money?

People often become funny when talking about money. Bringing up finances can cause people to get uncomfortable and clam up — especially in church. In some people's minds, money and church go together like whip cream and spaghetti. This is strange, considering that Jesus talked about money more than he did Heaven and Hell. In fact, he talked about money more than anything else except for the Kingdom of God.

Jesus understood that money is the way to our hearts — it determines our standard of living and what we can and can't do. Like it or not, we're married to it until we get to Heaven. Therefore, what we do with it reveals our motives and intentions — our hearts. Look what Jesus said:

> *Wherever your treasure is, there the desires of your heart will also be.*
> *-MATTHEW 6:21*

Because money tests our hearts, God watches how we handle it. He wants to see us put our money where our mouth is: do we serve God in word alone or are we happy to give him something that costs us something? Does money serve us or do we serve money? The only way God can know this is by examining whether or not we use it to help build his Kingdom upon the earth. If we do, we are telling God that his Kingdom is our first priority. And this pleases the Lord:

> *Seek the Kingdom of God above all else, and live righteously,*
> *and he will give you everything you need.*
> *—MATTHEW 6:33*

A big part of our heavenly reward is going to be based upon how we use our money to serve the Kingdom while we are alive. So, we'd better find out what the Bible tells us to do with it and how to do it with a cheerful heart:

> *To those who use well what they are given, even more will be*
> *given, and they will have an abundance. But from those who do*
> *nothing, even what little they have will be taken away.*
> *—MATTHEW 25:29*

Question 54: Why does God need my money?

God doesn't need your money, but *you need* to give it.

God has absolutely no need whatsoever. He is the Creator of all that is seen and unseen (Colossians 1:16); every animal in the forest is his and the cattle on a thousand hills belong to him (Psalm 50:10). It would be absurd to think that God is in need. So, when God tells us to give to him (Malachi 3:8-10), it isn't because *he* lacks anything.

The first reason that we need to give is because giving is a form of worship and an act of obedience. When we bring a portion of our earnings to God, we are acknowledging that we received it through God's strength, not our own. God wants to be our source and he asks us to worship him as such:

> *Yet for us there is [only] one God, the Father, Who is the Source of all things and for Whom we [have life], and one Lord, Jesus Christ, through and by Whom are all things and through and by Whom we [ourselves exist].*
> *-1 CORINTHIANS 8:6*

Another reason we need to give is because it takes money for God's work to get done. Church operations, missions, evangelism, caring for the poor, taking care of believers, etc. all require finances. Sure, God *could* make funds appear out of thin air. But that's now how he does it. He asks us to partner with him. This is a great privilege, and it comes with a blessing — God promises to take good care of his partners. Lending God our money always comes back with high yields. We can say that God is the best business partner we will ever have. His work is the only investment that *always* guarantees positive returns:

> *Remember this—a farmer who plants only a few seeds will get a small crop. But the one who plants generously will get a generous crop. You must each decide in your heart how much to give. And don't give reluctantly or in response to pressure. "For God loves a person who gives cheerfully." And God will generously provide all you need. Then you will always have everything you need and plenty left over to share with others. As the Scriptures say, "They share freely and give generously to the poor. Their good deeds will be remembered forever." For God is the one who provides seed for the farmer and then bread to eat. In the same way, he will provide and increase your resources and then produce a great harvest of generosity in you.*
> *-2 CORINTHIANS 9:6-10*

Finally, we give to God as an act of faith. It takes faith to trust God with what is most precious to us — our finances. Faith exercised through giving makes us God's responsibility. We don't need to be concerned with the ups and downs of the economy when our trust is in God. We have a partnership with Heaven that secures us supernatural provision in spite of any visible challenge:

*And it is impossible to please God without faith. Anyone
who wants to come to him must believe that God exists
and that he rewards those who sincerely seek him.*
—HEBREWS 11:6

Question 55: How much does God expect me to give him?

Now that we have established that we need to give to God, we need to determine how much.
According to Scripture, God asks us to give him *a tithe*:

*And all the tithe of the land, whether of the seed of the land, or of
the fruit of the tree, is the Lord's: it is holy unto the Lord.*
—LEVITICUS 27:30

The word tithe means *a tenth*. God has asked each of us to give him one tenth of what we've
earned. The first person to do this was Abraham (Genesis 14:19-20). Israel, under the Law of
Moses, practiced this as well (Numbers 18:21). And today, the Lord continues to receive our
tithes as we give to his work (Hebrews 7:8).

A tithe is not:

- Tipping God: Giving God a few dollars here and there.
- Giving out of guilt: Some only give to God because they feel guilty that it's been so
long since the last time they gave.
- Giving other things beside money: While it is great for us to give our time and energy
to the Kingdom of God, God expects us to give our money too. Thinking, *Well, I give
God this and that so I don't need to give my finances*, is trying to reason a way out of having to give to God financially. Remember, money is attached to our hearts. Holding
back our finances indicates a heart issue such as loving money more than God (1
Timothy 6:10) and failure to trust God.
- Donating: Donating means giving for a good cause. Very nice thing to do, but the
word does not capture the full essence of tithing. You see, many times people donate
their leftovers — perhaps an old bike, some worn clothes, a lamp from 1989. But
tithing is taking the first tenth of our earnings and presenting them before the Lord
because God deserves the best of the best. In fact, tithing is a covenant with God —
an agreement he will not break. God is so dedicated to this covenant that he chal-
lenges us to test him to see if he will not uphold his end of the covenant and bless us
for honoring him with the best of our earnings. Donating certainly doesn't have this
benefit:

*Bring all the tithes into the storehouse so there will be enough food in
my Temple. If you do," says the Lord of Heaven's Armies, "I will open*

the windows of heaven for you. I will pour out a blessing so great you
won't have enough room to take it in! Try it! Put me to the test!
-MALACHI 3:8-10

Beyond giving the tithe, God's Word teaches us to be generous. Generous means giving more than what is necessary or expected:

Remember this: Whoever sows sparingly will also reap sparingly,
and whoever sows generously will also reap generously.
-2 CORINTHIANS 9:6

A tenth is what is expected of us. But a tenth shouldn't be our limit. If the Holy Spirit moves upon our hearts to be generous, we should obey and go above our normal tithe. Giving above a tithe is called an offering (Deuteronomy 12:5-6).

Question 56: Where should I give?

Our tithes should be given to the local church that we are a part of — the one the Holy Spirit has led us to. The local church teaches us and our families the Word of God, ministers to our spiritual needs, provides oversight to our walk with Christ, and is also the place God has assigned us to do the work of the Kingdom. Naturally, this should be the place where we bring our financial support so that God's work can carry on. The Scripture teaches this:

Those who are taught the word of God should provide for
their teachers, sharing all good things with them.
—GALATIANS 6:6

Don't you realize that those who work in the temple get their meals from the
offerings brought to the temple? And those who serve at the altar get a share
of the sacrificial offerings. In the same way, the Lord ordered that those who
preach the Good News should be supported by those who benefit from it.
—1 CORINTHIANS 9:13-14

We certainly are allowed to give to other ministries, charities and benefits as God leads. However, we should never neglect supporting the local church because of its fundamental importance.

Question 57: How come it feels like all that preachers want is my money?

Let's get it out of the way and acknowledge that, yes, there are some preachers who *only* talk about money. However, they don't represent what the Word of God teaches, and they don't represent the majority of preachers. The majority of preachers are not driven by greed. In fact, most have made tremendous sacrifices to serve the Lord full time. It's unfair to bunch them up with a few spoiled eggs.

On the other hand, those who ask this question should search their own hearts to make certain that they aren't offended if preachers bring up money. Why shouldn't preachers talk about money? We like our church to be warm in winter, right? It's nice to have the lights on. It isn't so bad having comfortable seats to sit on. And isn't it a beautiful thing when the church is equipped with high-powered tech? Does God warm the sanctuary with his breath? Do angels show up at churches with a set of new computers and install them all for the price of lunch?

Pastors and churches use money like any other business. And the more income, the more a church can do and be. So why shouldn't a church ask the congregation to give, especially when the congregation is receiving so much from their church? Where do they make their Christian friends? Who teaches their children about Jesus? What place is there for them 24/7, 365? If we went anywhere else for this beside a church, we wouldn't wait to be asked before pulling out our wallets to pay for the services we benefited from receiving. Why is it different in church?

Most likely, it's the failure to consider spiritual things equal to natural things. *If it's from God, it must be free*, some people think. Yes, the Word of God is free. Salvation is free. The joy of the Lord is free. But what about the time the pastor spent preparing his sermon? Or the bricks it took to build the sanctuary? Those cost somebody something, didn't they? Doesn't God call all of us to help shoulder the burden? In fact, God's attitude is that pastors and ministers should be *paid well*. Isn't that something? God doesn't want his pastors to be just getting by. He wants them prosperous:

> *Elders who do their work well should be respected and paid well,*
> *especially those who work hard at both preaching and teaching.*
> —*1 TIMOTHY 5:17*

We can choose to take the attitude that we will give the church only what it absolutely needs, or we can take the attitude that if anyone deserves our money, it is our church and the ministers who look out for our souls. If you have a cheerful attitude about giving (which comes from a thankful heart), you'll never feel the preacher is asking for too much when he receives the tithes and offerings:

> *You must each decide in your heart how much to give. And don't give reluctantly*
> *or in response to pressure. "For God loves a person who gives cheerfully.*
> -*2 CORINTHIANS 9:7*

Question 58: Does God want me to be poor?
Absolutely not. No, no, and no. God wants you blessed, prosperous, and flourishing. Look:

Beloved, I wish above all things that thou mayest prosper
and be in health, even as thy soul prospereth.
—3 JOHN 2

Yes, you will be enriched in every way so that you can always be generous.
—2 CORINTHIANS 9:11A

We shouldn't feel guilty for having money and owning property. Even Jesus had a house (Mark 2:1-2). However, some read the New Testament and find stories of the apostles being persecuted and enduring tremendous suffering and then think this is God's will for every Christian. Persecution is the result of preaching God's Word where it isn't welcomed. But the majority of us now live in places where the Word of God has broken through and prevailed and is now enabling us to be prosperous. This is the reason God called for it to be preached in the first place — because his Word brings life and blessing:

So if the Son sets you free, you are truly free.
—JOHN 8:36

Those who suffered so that we could be free to prosper have a tremendous reward in store for them in Heaven (Revelation 20:4). Let's not think that we owe it to them to suffer in order to recompense them for their sacrifices — only God can repay them. What we *can* do in return is use our prosperity to help the Gospel be preached, so that future generations can prosper. We can also support missions in other places where the Gospel is not welcomed, like Muslim, Hindu, and Communist nations:

And you will know the truth, and the truth will set you free.
—JOHN 8:32

Question 59: I already have wealth. Why do I need God?

It's possible to build our own empires without the help of God's blessing. A little business savvy, a bit of charisma, a lot of determination, and some good old-fashioned luck can put a whole lot of cash into our pockets. Think of all the millionaires and billionaires who have prospered without God: it can be done. But Jesus told us it's a bad idea:

And what do you benefit if you gain the whole world but lose your own soul?
—MARK 8:36

A person who does not use their money to help God fails to build wealth *in Heaven*. When they die and their riches fail, they'll have nothing waiting for them in eternity. What an empty feeling it would be to stand before God and hear him say that our heavenly account is empty.

But the Bible teaches that if we use our money to help God, we won't have anything to fear when our riches fail:

The blessing of the Lord makes a person rich, and he adds no sorrow with it.
—Proverbs 10:22

This is because when we help God with our money, we are establishing eternal wealth — literally investing in eternity and creating a heavenly legacy. When we die, we will have the gains of our heavenly investments to look forward to:

Don't store up treasures here on earth, where moths eat them and rust destroys
them, and where thieves break in and steal. Store your treasures in heaven,
where moths and rust cannot destroy, and thieves do not break in and steal.
—Matthew 6:19-20

Here's the lesson: Use your worldly resources to benefit others and make friends.
Then, when your possessions are gone, they will welcome you to an eternal home.
—Luke 16:9

CHAPTER 11

Can't I Just Let Preachers Tell People About Jesus?

Let's go back in time. Think about the exact moment you gave your life to Jesus. Imagine again the quilt of peace that overlaid your soul and warmed your heart. Reflect on that mysterious assurance which took hold of your hope and guaranteed you a life past death. Where were you? What year was it? What were you doing? And for the sake of this discussion, *who* told you?

We forget a lot of people throughout life, but never those who played a part in leading us to Christ. It could have been a janitor who cornered you in the lunch room while you ate your sandwich, or the neighboring locker at the gym, perhaps even a virtual friend you know from Facebook (whom you *still* haven't met face to face). Whoever they are, and wherever they might be, they hold a special place in your heart because they cared enough to let you in on some Good News.

Receiving the Good News is the only way we can be saved. But we never would have heard it if, let's say, the janitor decided that eating his lunch was more important than sharing with you. In other words, God's message of salvation only goes as far as the people who are willing to share it:

> *But how can they call on him to save them unless they believe in him? And how can they believe in him if they have never heard about him? And how can they hear about him unless someone tells them? And how will anyone go and tell them without being sent?*
> —ROMANS 10:14-15

Sharing the Gospel is another area where God has asked us to partner with him for the sake of his Kingdom. And this invitation isn't to full time pastors only. It is for all those who have Good News to share. In fact, Christianity spread so fast in the first century because its followers were driven to share the Gospel. And the apostles weren't the only ones doing the work. Fishermen, craftsmen, traders, merchants, moneychangers, sailors, soldiers, and market traders were all passing the message on to one another. God knew what he was doing when he told all of his followers:

> *Go into all the world and preach the Good News to everyone. Anyone*
> *who believes and is baptized will be saved. But anyone who refuses*
> *to believe will be condemned. These miraculous signs will accompany*
> *those who believe: They will cast out demons in my name, and they will*
> *speak in new languages. They will be able to handle snakes with safety,*
> *and if they drink anything poisonous, it won't hurt them. They will*
> *be able to place their hands on the sick, and they will be healed.*
> *—MARK 16:15-18*

Jesus's command makes everyone of us a preacher.

Question 60: Won't people dislike me if I tell them about Jesus?

Maybe; maybe not. The important thing is being willing to share the Gospel, despite what people think, because it's the right thing to do. If we believe the Scripture, then we believe that there *is* eternal separation from God in Hell and the *only* way to be saved from it is through Jesus (Acts 4:12). Holding back the news is like withholding medicine from the terminally ill.

When the Holy Spirit empowers your life, you will receive a passion to share the Good News — even more than a passion: a fire. Fire is passion with urgency. Eternity awaits; it's just a heartbeat away for us all. Therefore, the fire of God never wastes a moment or lets an opportunity escape. It can't — a person's eternity is at risk!

So who cares what people think? Despite our fire and passion, there will always be those who won't like what we have to say. Their hearts are hard and they are blind toward the truth because Satan has them bound:

> *Satan, who is the god of this world, has blinded the minds of*
> *those who don't believe. They are unable to see the glorious light*
> *of the Good News. They don't understand this message about*
> *the glory of Christ, who is the exact likeness of God.*
> *—2 CORINTHIANS 4:4*

These individuals may end up reacting with persecution, which is hostile treatment toward the Gospel and those who proclaim it. The different kinds of persecution vary. In early Christianity it was often a shameful, tormenting death: believers were impaled on posts after their hair was dipped in tar and their heads lit on fire in order to serve as torches along the main roads. And, believe it or not, brutality like this still exists toward Christians in Muslim and Communist countries. In free countries, the persecution is much lighter, but still no fun: being branded the weird guy at work, losing friends, missing opportunities for promotion, etc. And, rest assured, as "Christian" societies move farther and farther away from God, hostility toward Christians will become more and more frequent. But God tells us to endure it, we, the soldiers of Christ. Our lives' mission isn't to win a popularity contest. We are here to reconcile people to God:

*Endure suffering along with me, as a good soldier of Christ
Jesus. Soldiers don't get tied up in the affairs of civilian life, for
then they cannot please the officer who enlisted them.*
—2 TIMOTHY 2:3-4

Question 61: People should believe what they want. Why bother good people?

Some consider it rude to share the Gospel. They cringe at the thought of telling a "good" person that they are going to Hell unless they accept Jesus. *Why can't we just leave them alone,* they wonder. *They are good people and aren't harming anyone.* But a person who rejects Jesus isn't good.

Good is a relative term among humanity. People have their own ideas of what is good: going green to save the planet, protesting women's rights for equal pay, discovering ways to save businesses money, fighting for their countries' freedom, feeding the poor. Sure, these are noble and virtuous. But none of them is the *source* of good. Jesus taught that *he alone* is the source of good and, unless we give up everything to follow him, we can never be "good":

"Why do you call me good?" Jesus asked. "Only God is truly good.
—MARK 10:18

So while people set up their own standard of good, God tells us that good is following him. And he bids us:

Come, follow me.
—MARK 10:21

So when we tell others about Jesus, we are inviting people who are eager to do good to discover the source of goodness: Jesus. What's wrong with that?

Question 62: How do I tell people about Jesus?

Life is full of opportunities to share our faith and tell others about Jesus. When they come, we must snatch them up. Here are a few ways to do just that:

- Pray for the opportunities: Opportunities come when we pray for them. Ask the Lord to send you divine appointments — situations that take place because God set them up.

So pray to the Lord who is in charge of the harvest; ask
him to send more workers into his fields.
—MATTHEW 9:38

- Be prepared: We need to be ready at all times. A sharp sword cuts faster and deeper than a dull sword. Memorize Scriptures and stay full of the Spirit. Also, it's important to stay up-to-date with current events. Being in touch with the latest proves that the Gospel is applicable today. And finally, bone up on what others believe. If you are around Muslims, you should be familiar with what they believe and be ready to answer them. The same goes for atheists, Hindus, and every other belief contrary to Christ.

> *Instead, you must worship Christ as Lord of your life. And if someone asks about your hope as a believer, always be ready to explain it.*
> *—1 PETER 3:15-16*

- Be tasteful: Sharing the Gospel should never be done in anger, out of force, with impatience, or in pride. Furthermore, we should be wise about timing: there are times and places to share, and times and places where sharing won't be fruitful. As messengers, we should always do our best to validate the message we are speaking — being appropriate helps.

> *A servant of the Lord must not quarrel but must be kind to everyone, be able to teach, and be patient with difficult people.*
> *—2 TIMOTHY 2:24*

- Minister to a need: Everyone has a need. Could be inner healing, deliverance from an obsessive habit, healing of sickness, counsel for a situation, comfort during a hard time, etc. Find the person's need and introduce them to the One who can supply it.

> *And this same God who takes care of me will supply all your needs from his glorious riches, which have been given to us in Christ Jesus.*
> *—PHILIPPIANS 4:19*

- Tell your testimony: Nobody can argue with your personal experience. Who can deny what has happened to you? Your personal encounter with Jesus will carry a weight of conviction unlike anything else. Share it and share it often.

> *And they have defeated him by the blood of the Lamb and by their testimony.*
> *—REVELATION 12:11*

- Offer to pray: People rarely turn down prayer. Tell the person you are ministering to about God's power, his willingness to deliver and heal, and about God's never-failing love. Get them in a position to expect something good from God, and then pray over their life. If they need salvation, lead them in the sinner's prayer like the one you prayed when you gave your life to Jesus.

> For "Everyone who calls on the name of the Lord will be saved."
> —ROMANS 10:13

CHAPTER 12

How Should I Treat Others?

The Christian life is a race we run alongside one other. Unity is the heart of God. So much so, actually, just before Jesus went to the cross, he prayed that his followers would live in concord. This was Christ's dying request!

> *I pray that they will all be one, just as you and I are one—*
> *as you are in me, Father, and I am in you. And may they*
> *be in us so that the world will believe you sent me.*
> *—JOHN 17:21*

Unity isn't something that just happens, however. Now matter how long we have been Christians, we need to deliberately work at getting along. And God's Word is full of Scriptures that teach us. It tells us how to treat one another with love (1 Corinthians 13), resolve conflict (Matthew 18:15-17), take interest in each other (Philippians 2:4), and even how we should communicate together (Colossians 4:6). Unless we plan on living in a cave (which God wouldn't want to see us do), we can trust God's Word to give us the wisdom to live in harmony with each other:

> *Work at living in peace with everyone, and work at living a holy life,*
> *for those who are not holy will not see the Lord. Look after each other*
> *so that none of you fails to receive the grace of God. Watch out that no*
> *poisonous root of bitterness grows up to trouble you, corrupting many.*
> *—HEBREWS 12:14-15*

Question 63: I don't like other Christians. Is that OK?

No, it's not OK.

Though few might actually ask this question, there *are* those who feel this way. Within, they aren't fond of other Christians and — even though they are one — have all kinds of issues with them. If these feelings aren't dealt with, they will turn the individual who feels them to the world for friendships and relationships. They will become heavily influenced and, eventually, this person will leave Christianity altogether. Happens all the time.

But other Christians are not the problem. When a Christian doesn't like other Christians, their own bitterness is usually the problem. Notice:

> *Look after each other so that none of you fails to receive the grace of God. Watch out that no poisonous root of bitterness grows up to trouble you, corrupting many.*
> —*HEBREWS 12:15*

A lemon is a perfect example of bitterness: it lacks sweetness, is sour, and tearing off a bite is unpleasant even to imagine. A bitter Christian is no more pleasant to be around than a mouthful of ripe citrus: their words are sharp, their attitude is cynical, and they are filled with contempt. Rest assured, this person has been wounded. While following Christ, they've experienced hardship or failure, jealousy or disappointment, neglect or abandonment, and they did not deal with it properly. Now, they have been corrupted and are blaming other Christians for it.

Corrupt describes a person with raging emotions and rotten speech — the result of feeling that they have been treated unfairly. They were offended by a Christian, took it personally, and the wound festered and turned into gangrene of the soul. As it spreads, it ruins their opinions of the Church. Left untreated, the gangrene will take hold of their understanding of God's Word and ultimately their understanding of Jesus.

As we follow Christ, experiencing wounds and disappointments will be normal. We can expect the time to come when another Christian, perhaps even a pastor or leader, will offend us. But Jesus said this would happen:

> *Then said he unto the disciples, It is impossible but that offences will come: but woe unto him, through whom they come!*
> —*LUKE 17:1*

Christians aren't perfect. We are all growing in the Lord and make mistakes along the way — even hurtful ones. But we must be understanding and quick to issue forgiveness, lest bitterness spoils our love for one another and turns us from Christ:

> *Make allowance for each other's faults, and forgive anyone who offends you. Remember, the Lord forgave you, so you must forgive others.*
> —*COLOSSIANS 3:13*

Question 64: Only God can judge others, right?

We hear it said all the time, "Only God can judge me!" (Especially when someone is doing something they should be ashamed of.) Is this true? Is *God* the only person who can judge? Some use Jesus's words in Matthew 7:1, to say it's so:

Do not judge others, and you will not be judged.
—MATTHEW 7:1

But is Jesus saying that we should never judge, ever? That would be difficult to believe, considering the Bible commends using good judgment (Psalm 119:66). So what did Jesus mean? We need to understand the context.

Jesus is in the middle of warning against hypocrisy. He had just cautioned about giving, praying, and fasting the way the hypocrites do (Matthew 6) and then he tackles the issue of judging, saying:

> *And why worry about a speck in your friend's eye when you have a log in your own? How can you think of saying to your friend, 'Let me help you get rid of that speck in your eye,' when you can't see past the log in your own eye? Hypocrite! First get rid of the log in your own eye; then you will see well enough to deal with the speck in your friend's eye.*
> —MATTHEW 7:3-5

Jesus is not telling us that we should never judge; he is telling us we are never to judge indiscriminately and sanctimoniously.

The truth is, God's Word tells us that there are times where we will *have* to judge. Notice:

> *It isn't my responsibility to judge outsiders, but it certainly is your responsibility to judge those inside the church who are sinning. God will judge those on the outside; but as the Scriptures say, "You must remove the evil person from among you."*
> —1 CORINTHIANS 5:12-13

Here, a church is being told to correct the immorality of one of its members. This particular man was having illicit sex and was not sorry about it. It was starting to affect the church negatively. God's solution? Remove him:

> *I can hardly believe the report about the sexual immorality going on among you—something that even pagans don't do. I am told that a man in your church is living in sin with his stepmother. You are so proud of yourselves, but you should be mourning in sorrow and shame. And you should remove this man from your fellowship.*
> —1 CORINTHIANS 5:1-2

How could the church remove him unless they first judged him? And mind you, these were imperfect people doing the judging. They used to live sinfully, themselves (1 Corinthians 6:11).

Only now they were striving to please the Lord. Therefore, God gave them the right to judge the shameless man's actions and remove him from their pursuit of holiness.

The Scripture also tells us to be careful whom we hang out with:

> Don't be fooled by those who say such things, for
> "bad company corrupts good character."
> —1 CORINTHIANS 15:33

How can we decide on the difference between good friends and bad friends unless we use judgment?

Furthermore, the apostle Paul warned Titus that the people of Crete were dishonest and lazy. He told Titus to reprimand them for it:

> Even one of their own men, a prophet from Crete, has said about them,
> "The people of Crete are all liars, cruel animals, and lazy gluttons." This
> is true. So reprimand them sternly to make them strong in the faith.
> —TITUS 1:12-13

Isn't this judging? Of course it is. And there is nothing wrong with it when it's being done with the right intentions and with the right heart. Here are a few things that ensure judging is done correctly:

- It's actually our business to judge: God forbids us to get involved in things that don't concern us (1 Corinthians 5:12).
- We have the authority to judge: It is wrong for us to attempt to exercise authority we don't have. For instance, if a pastor has erred, it isn't a member's job to put them in their place. The pastor's elders, the church board, or whomever he or she considers their spiritual covering should do this.
- We are using judgment to help and not harm: Judgment should go toward helping the overall greater good of those involved and, if possible, restoring the person who is wrong.
- Love: In everything, we should show love by believing the best and hoping for the best.

Question 65: Can I take revenge?

Not a chance. God does not give us permission anywhere in the Bible to return harm to someone for a wrong they have caused. When Jesus became Lord of our lives, we relinquished our right to seek justice for ourselves and turned it over to him. Notice:

> Dear friends, never take revenge. Leave that to the righteous anger of God. For
> the Scriptures say, "I will take revenge; I will pay them back," says the Lord.
> —ROMANS 12:19

Now, we practice forgiveness — and it's not always easy. Our flesh wants to see our offender suffer so they can feel what they have put us through — so we can say, "See! Now you know how it feels!" But God promises us that if we leave it in his hands, we will end up with so much more; we will come away with his blessings.

Question 66: I have some juicy dirt. Can I share it?

Dirt, chatter, blabber. It's all the same — the Bible calls it foul language and warns us not to use it:

> *Don't use foul or abusive language. Let everything you say be good and helpful,*
> *so that your words will be an encouragement to those who hear them.*
> —*Ephesians 4:29*

Foul language refers to speech that is full of disease. These aren't only cuss words — there are three other types of speech that qualify as putrid, decaying, and useless talk:

- Backbiting: This is speaking derogatorily about someone when they aren't present (2 Corinthians 12:20).
- Whispering: This is secretly passing information along about someone else. It often begins with, "Keep this between us…" (2 Corinthians 12:20).
- Gossip: This is talking mindlessly about meaningless things. It includes spreading rumors, chatting about other people's business, speaking like an authority on matters that we have no accurate information about, and repeating hearsay (1 Timothy 5:12-13).

Foul language has devastating effects. It:

- Blemishes our view of the person being discussed: Once we form an impression of someone, it's hard to get rid of it even if it's not accurate (Colossians 3:8).
- Destroys people's trust: Gossipers can't be trusted. When we spot one, we distance ourselves from them because they are liable to talk about anyone, including us (Proverbs 20:19).
- Creates an environment where foul language is accepted: By entertaining someone's gossip, we are approving them to continue with it and come to us with more gossip next time around (Proverbs 26:20).
- Causes division: When whisperings and backbiting go on, people soon take sides (Proverbs 16:28).
- Angers people: Think of a time when you heard someone being talked about unfairly. How did you feel? It's probable that you resented the gossiper for it (Proverbs 25:23).
- Grieves the Holy Spirit: When God hears us talking bad about each other, it devastates him and breaks his heart (Ephesians 4:30).

You're best leaving gossip alone. You desire a peaceful life, yes? Then don't throw dirt; don't talk foul. Remember, God said:

> *I will not tolerate people who slander their neighbors.*
> *I will not endure conceit and pride.*
> *—PSALM 101:5*

CHAPTER 13

How Does God Expect Me to Live?

God's not trying to take away our fun and he doesn't sit around thinking of ways to make our lives boring. Unfortunately, many believe that serving God is a drag and don't serve him because they figure his rules will cut into their personal enjoyment. That's a lie from Satan.

God gives us his rules because his rules protect us from sin — and sin leads to death:

> *For the wages of sin is death, but the free gift of God is*
> *eternal life through Christ Jesus our Lord.*
> *—Romans 6:23*

There's an old saying: *Sin will take you farther than you want to go, keep you longer than you want to stay, and cost you more than you want to pay.* God loves you and doesn't want to ever watch you go through the horrors of sin, so he issues a strong warning about it.

Can you think of a time when someone you know was busted for doing something wrong? Not just a criminal — perhaps someone who was sneaking around and cheating on their spouse or lying about a situation until it caught up with them? Know anyone who's made a series of poor choices that caused them mental and emotional damage in the long run? Sin leads to a difficult and complicated life:

> *The way of transgressors is hard.*
> *—Proverbs 13:15b*

Hence, God desires us to be separate from sin, not just for his sake, but for our sakes as well:

> *Therefore, come out from among unbelievers, and separate yourselves from*
> *them, says the Lord. Don't touch their filthy things, and I will welcome you.*
> *—2 Corinthians 6:17*

A life that's not mingled with sin is peaceful and undisturbed. Who doesn't want that? Think of going to bed at night and being able to sleep because you aren't afraid of being exposed. Imagine being able to look people in the eye because you haven't done them any wrong. Picture being alone with your thoughts and enjoying them because they aren't haunted by the memories of sinful experiences. You can secure that with holiness, the standard of behavior for God's people.

Holiness isn't just a set of restrictions; it's living like God. Who can say their state of living is better than God's? When we live like God, we will be just as healthy and alive as he is. Isn't that an amazing thought? Life — the way God has it. You might think this is impossible, but God said it isn't. He lives inside of us now, remember? We can do it!

> *Work at living in peace with everyone, and work at living a*
> *holy life, for those who are not holy will not see the Lord.*
> —*HEBREWS 12:14*

Holiness is liberating. Through it, we throw off the junky habits, the disabling addictions, the cruddy lifestyle — and we take up the life of God:

> *Because we have these promises, dear friends, let us cleanse*
> *ourselves from everything that can defile our body or spirit. And*
> *let us work toward complete holiness because we fear God.*
> —*2 CORINTHIANS 7:1*

So when God tells us to do something, we can trust it's for our good. And we'll be glad we listened.

Question 67: Why can't I have sex before marriage?

Ah, the big question. If anything seems unappealing about obeying God, it's saving sex for marriage. *Who wants to do that?* we may think. *One of the great joys of life is having sex, and God wants to cut that off?*

Nope, not at all. God actually wants to enhance your sex life, you know, make it better than you could ever imagine. And he knows how to do it. After all, he invented sex, didn't he? A fulfilling sex life is not about spicing it up the way magazines at the supermarket checkout counter tell us to. And it sure isn't about trying out new partners until we find an explosive chemistry. These are the world's solutions. And have you stopped to notice how broken-hearted the world is?

There is an explanation for the heartbreak that comes from promiscuous sex. The Bible shares it with us, and it tips us off why sex before marriage is a bad idea:

> *Don't you realize that your bodies are actually parts of Christ? Should a man take his body, which is part of Christ, and join it to a prostitute? Never! And don't you realize that if a man joins himself to a prostitute, he becomes one body with her? For the Scriptures say, "The two are united into one." But the person who is joined to the Lord is one spirit with him. Run from sexual sin! No other sin so clearly affects the body as this one does. For sexual immorality is a sin against your own body.*
> *—1 CORINTHIANS 6:15-18*

Sex attaches us to one another. It's a bond that makes us one with our partner. That bond isn't broken until death. Much more than just a physical union, sex weaves our souls together. This explains why people feel attached to their partner after they've had sex. In fact, there are times when they feel each other's presence when they aren't around one other. They are one and their souls are tied so they cannot escape.

A soul-tie is a spiritual, emotional, mental, or physical attachment that connects two people. A soul-tie:

- Causes bad judgment: Perhaps the relationship was abusive or just the wrong thing. A soul-tie keeps couples in the relationship when they should get out.
- Produces irrational thinking: A soul-tie will make people read into things that just aren't so. For instance, if someone wants to get back together with their partner, they may take every little thing as a sign that the relationship is going to be restored.
- Creates unhealthy attractions: If someone can't have the person they are tied to, they may end up looking for someone like that person. This often turns into disaster.

The only way a soul-tie is broken is through repentance, which leads to inner healing (Romans 10:13). But there is no need for deliverance if we just obey God and reserve sex for the place God gives it in marriage. And God sure does give it a great place.

The Song of Songs says a lot about what God thinks of sex. It's an intimate exchange between a married couple and contains verses about a sweet, luscious, and fulfilling sex life. It's true love — committed and sacred — aflame with passion and romance. Listen to this:

> *Your breasts are like two fawns, twin fawns of a gazelle grazing among the lilies.*
> *—SONG OF SOLOMON 4:5*

Talk about amatory! And the best thing about it is that this couple never deals with breaking up and going through the bitterness of extinguishing their love:

> *Now regarding the questions you asked in your letter. Yes, it is good to abstain from sexual relations. But because there is so much sexual immorality, each man should have his own wife, and each woman should have her own husband.*
> *—1 CORINTHIANS 7:1-2*

Question 68: So what if I sin? God will forgive me anyway, right?

God is forgiving, absolutely. But God only issues forgiveness when we're *truly* sorry:

> *But if we confess our sins to him, he is faithful and just to*
> *forgive us our sins and to cleanse us from all wickedness.*
> *—1 JOHN 1:9*

Sorrow is reflected within our attitude toward sin. True sorrow:

- Grieves us: We regret what we have done and wish we had never done it.
- Disappoints us: We are frustrated for letting God down.
- Inspires us: We are serious about changing and not repeating the same sin.

When our attitude is like this, God can help us. Notice:

> *For the kind of sorrow God wants us to experience leads us away from*
> *sin and results in salvation. There's no regret for that kind of sorrow. But*
> *worldly sorrow, which lacks repentance, results in spiritual death.*
> *—2 CORINTHIANS 7:10*

However, true sorrow is not premeditated sin. Premeditated sin is the attitude *sin now and ask for forgiveness later*. This doesn't reflect someone who is truly sorry, and most importantly, it doesn't reflect someone who really cares about pleasing God — it reflects someone trying to take advantage of God's forgiveness. God's goodness should cause us to serve him with honor and humility, not self-interest and entitlement:

> *Work hard to show the results of your salvation,*
> *obeying God with deep reverence and fear.*
> *—PHILIPPIANS 2:12*

So, experiencing God's forgiveness has more to do with our attitude than it does with whether or not God wants to forgive us.

Question 69: Isn't it impossible to resist temptation?

If we are in Christ, sin has no control over us — it cannot force us against our will — no matter how strong the temptation to sin might be:

> *Sin is no longer your master, for you no longer live under the requirements*
> *of the law. Instead, you live under the freedom of God's grace.*
> *—ROMANS 6:14*

God has given us all the power we need to resist temptation and escape it. He has done his part:

> *No temptation has overtaken you except what is common to mankind. And God*
> *is faithful; he will not let you be tempted beyond what you can bear. But when*
> *you are tempted, he will also provide a way out so that you can endure it.*
> —*1 CORINTHIANS 10:13*

So whether or not we sin comes down to our own wills. Do we want to give in or not? It's a decision we make. And our decision depends on how strong a will we have against sin.

A strong will against sin is developed by having strong, daily time with the Lord. This includes praying in the Spirit, renewing the mind by reading and studying God's Word, and making God's Word a priority to obey. The more we practice this, the more we will love what is right and hate what is not, and the easier it becomes to say *no* to sin (Romans 12:9).

If we notice that our passions for sin have come alive and that temptation is becoming more enticing, it's a clear indication that our daily time with the Lord is lacking and needs to improve. Jesus likened our spiritual walk to a vine and a branch. Just as the branch needs the vine in order to receive life and strength, so we need fellowship with Jesus. Without it, we will wither:

> *I am the vine; you are the branches. If you remain in me and I in you,*
> *you will bear much fruit; apart from me you can do nothing.*
> —*JOHN 15:5*

Question 70: Will God send me to Hell if I make a mistake?

There is no need to fear Hell if you are a born again, dear child of God — even if you make a mistake and sin. You have received the Lord Jesus as your Savior and have become part of God's family. Missing the mark here and there is not enough to get you expelled from the family of God. Certainly your Heavenly Father's mercy reaches past a mistake.

Now, some of the differences between us who have accepted Jesus and those who have rejected Jesus are: 1. *how often* we sin and 2. *our attitude* when we sin. For us, sin shouldn't be an everyday thing; it should be as foreign to us as trying to speak another language. In other words, it shouldn't be comfortable and shouldn't come easy — it's not part of our nature! When we sin, it will feel wrong, we will feel out of place, and we will seek the Lord for forgiveness and correction. But sin is as natural as drinking water for those who have rejected Jesus — it's constant and done without second thought.

Essentially, Christians aren't habitual sinners. If you are habitually sinning, you may have to question whether or not you have truly been saved. It's a sobering thought. However, Jesus told us that we would know a tree by its fruit:

You can identify them by their fruit, that is, by the way they act.
Can you pick grapes from thornbushes, or figs from thistles?
—MATTHEW 7:16

For those who *have* been saved, the only way to become in danger of going to Hell is through a conscious choice to reject Jesus. This is possible:

For it is impossible to bring back to repentance those who were once
enlightened—those who have experienced the good things of heaven and shared
in the Holy Spirit, who have tasted the goodness of the word of God and the
power of the age to come—and who then turn away from God. It is impossible to
bring such people back to repentance; by rejecting the Son of God, they themselves
are nailing him to the cross once again and holding him up to public shame.
—HEBREWS 6:4-6

Of course, deciding to reject Jesus after following him is an issue of the heart. A choice like this doesn't happen overnight. It happens over time, as Satan works to deceive and mix up the truth about Christ:

The seed that fell on the footpath represents those who hear the message
about the Kingdom and don't understand it. Then the evil one comes
and snatches away the seed that was planted in their hearts.
—MATTHEW 13:18

As long as we guard our hearts and quickly repent for wrongdoing, we have nothing to fear.

Question 71: What should I do if I make a mistake?

It's very simple: when you make a mistake, ask the Lord to forgive you. Notice:

But if we confess our sins to him, he is faithful and just to
forgive us our sins and to cleanse us from all wickedness.
—1 JOHN 1:9

It's absurd to think that if we sin we don't need to ask God for forgiveness. Sin displeases God and causes him sorrow; it grieves him:

And do not bring sorrow to God's Holy Spirit by the way you live.
—EPHESIANS 4:30

So after we've sinned, it's our responsibility to acknowledge that we have caused God sorrow and to seek his mercy.

Sinning as a Christian, however, does not disrupt our legal status before God. We are still part of his family, though we have done wrong. Asking God for forgiveness is similar to a child approaching a loving father when they have disobeyed. Though the father isn't pleased, he doesn't expel his child from the house or torture them so they learn a tougher lesson. He may correct them or allow them to experience the consequences of their disobedience, but he still has their best interests at heart and, most importantly, he still loves and cherishes them.

You can trust, that if you are sorry for your sin, God will forgive you and restore any disruption that sin has caused your spiritual life. The Bible says that Jesus is our Advocate: he personally takes our plea before God and secures forgiveness for us. All we need to do is ask:

> *My dear children, I am writing this to you so that you will not sin.*
> *But if anyone does sin, we have an advocate who pleads our case before*
> *the Father. He is Jesus Christ, the one who is truly righteous.*
> *—1 John 2:1*

CHAPTER 14

Does God Heal?

Sickness is an enemy. For as long as the human race has existed, it has ravaged the population, bringing pain and death. Medicine has worked relentlessly to defeat this foe, improving by leaps-and-bounds as days go by. But despite the great advances made into the 21st century, sickness still kills. It doesn't seem that there will ever be a way to eliminate it, once and for all — at least, not now.

The Bible calls sickness an enemy — and not just an enemy — but oppression of the devil:

> *And you know that God anointed Jesus of Nazareth with the Holy*
> *Spirit and with power. Then Jesus went around doing good and healing*
> *all who were oppressed by the devil, for God was with him.*
> *—Acts 10:38*

Sickness is the malevolent weapon of Satan, used to afflict the world with sorrow, sadness, and agony. Satan has the ability to deploy his weapon because the earth is currently under his control; the Bible calls him the god of this world (2 Corinthians 4:4). He is still at work upon the earth trying to establish his kingdom. And because his judgment has not yet come, he does what he can to prevent it (Revelation 12:12). This includes inflicting the world with sickness.

Yet, sickness isn't *just* a direct result of Satan; it's also the result of a fallen world due to sin. Though Jesus declared that his Kingdom has come (Luke 17:20-21), his Kingdom has not *fully* been established (Luke 19:11-27); it's in the process. Until it has fully been set up, sickness will continue to run its course. There will come a day, however, when Jesus will return and he will put a final end to sickness and sin (Revelation 21:4).

Finally, sickness is the result of demons. Demons are the minions of Satan who harass human beings. Many times, the New Testament shows them using sickness to do so:

One Sabbath day as Jesus was teaching in a synagogue, he saw a woman who had been crippled by an evil spirit. She had been bent double for eighteen years and was unable to stand up straight. When Jesus saw her, he called her over and said, "Dear woman, you are healed of your sickness!" Then he touched her, and instantly she could stand straight. How she praised God!
—Luke 13:10-13

During his ministry on the earth, Jesus always opposed sickness — he worked to destroy it (1 John 3:8). This is why we find him in the Bible healing everyone who came to him (Matthew 15:30). Never do we find him putting sickness on people or issuing it as a blessing from God. He was compassionate to those who were sick and worked tirelessly to make people well. For this reason, we know it is the will of God to heal, even today. Jesus has not changed: he is the same yesterday, today, and forever (Hebrews 13:8). He still sees sickness in the same way and wants us to treat it the way he did (Mark 16:15-18).

Question 72: Does God make people sick so they can learn a lesson?

Jesus was the will of God in action. His entire ministry was devoted to healing people and making them well. Therefore, it's outrageous to believe that God would ever put sickness on people for any purpose, even to teach a lesson. Whatever comes from God is good and perfect. This is what the book of James tells us:

Whatever is good and perfect is a gift coming down to us from God our Father, who created all the lights in the heavens. He never changes or casts a shifting shadow.
—James 1:17

Sickness isn't good, is it? Is disease? Of course not! Therefore, God doesn't go around handing it out.

Now, certainly God does allow sickness to happen. In Job's case, he allowed it. But it wasn't God who made him sick — Satan did (Job 2:4-7). Yet, despite his suffering, Job got well. And not only did he get well, he ended up better off than before he was sick:

When Job prayed for his friends, the Lord restored his fortunes. In fact, the Lord gave him twice as much as before!
—Isaiah 42:10

Just because God allows something to happen doesn't mean he desires it or that it's even his perfect will. And this is certainly true when it comes to sickness: it's never God's perfect will for our lives and he will never make us sick. God's will is for us to be blessed, healthy, and full of life:

Dear friend, I hope all is well with you and that you are
as healthy in body as you are strong in spirit.
—3 John 2

Question 73: Does God want to heal me?

Nobody ever doubts that God *can* heal; they doubt if he *wants* to heal. The best way to settle this question is to look at Jesus. Remember, he was the will of God in action. When we read about the life and ministry of Jesus, it seems that he is always on his way to heal people. This makes sense, though. He was sent for that purpose:

Jesus saw the huge crowd as he stepped from the boat, and
he had compassion on them and healed their sick.
—Matthew 14:14

He sent out his word and healed them, snatching them from the door of death.
—Psalm 107:20

So one of the reasons Jesus came was to heal. Thinking that God doesn't *want* to heal us is just not Scriptural, as proved by the life of Jesus. It's a belief unfounded in something other than God's Word. It could come from:

- Feeling guilty and unworthy of God's healing power.
- Incorrect teaching.
- False humility — thinking sickness glorifies God.
- Believing God is cruel.
- Trying to earn healing.
- Losing someone to sickness.

Be as it may, Jesus came down to earth and did what he wanted to do: he healed. We should accept this and not try to make it any more complicated than it is: God's will is healing.

Question 74: I am sick. What should I do?

Though God doesn't want to see people sick, it happens. Thankfully, God's Word teaches us how to reach out to God for healing. If we get sick, no matter how small or great that sickness might be, we should:

- Believe it's God's will to heal: Our faith moves God (Hebrews 11:6). Again, faith is total and complete trust in the Lord. Faith for healing, then, is total and complete trust that God can heal us and that he will heal us.

- Speak God's Word over your life: Speaking God's Word and agreeing with it exercises our faith. Jesus told us that there is tremendous power in doing this.

> *Then Jesus said to the disciples, "Have faith in God. I tell you the truth, you can say to this mountain, 'May you be lifted up and thrown into the sea,' and it will happen. But you must really believe it will happen and have no doubt in your heart. I tell you, you can pray for anything, and if you believe that you've received it, it will be yours.*
> —*MARK 11:22-24*

- Don't focus on your symptoms: That's not to deny that you are having them — rather, keep your eyes centered on the truth that God has provided healing through Jesus and declare that healing over your body.

> *The tongue can bring death or life.*
> —*PROVERBS 18:21*

- Don't fear: Resist the urge to fear. Don't pay attention to the outcome that others who shared the same sickness had. Don't pay attention to statistics. Don't pay attention to what medical science can and can't do. You serve the God of the miraculous.
- Thank God: God has already provided healing through Jesus. In other words, everything that God needs to do in order to heal your body has been done. The right response to something that God has already done is thankfulness!

> *He personally carried our sins in his body on the cross so that we can be dead to sin and live for what is right. By his wounds you are healed.*
> —*1 PETER 2:24*

> *Be thankful in all circumstances, for this is God's will for you who belong to Christ Jesus.*
> —*1 THESSALONIANS 5:18*

- Be patient and don't give up: Healing doesn't always happen instantly. It can and does, but it's not always the case. Stay in faith and don't cast away your confidence that God will heal you. Faith in God requires patience, but that patience always brings about a great reward.

> *Who through faith and patience inherit the promises.*
> —*HEBREWS 6:12B*

- Have a pastor or a leader from your church lay hands on you and anoint you with oil: God's healing power is a tangible substance. On one occasion, it flowed through the hem of Jesus's garment and into a woman who couldn't stop bleeding — and the woman was healed (Luke 8:46). That same healing power is able to flow through his servants' hands today because God has chosen his servants' hands to be vessels of his healing (Mark 16:18). Therefore, God tells the sick to call for a pastor or a leader from their church and to receive laying on of hands and anointing with oil. (The oil is not the agent whereby we are healed. It's just symbolic of healing, as sicknesses were often treated with oil during the days of the New Testament. So, it represents God's healing power that has been released and is at work.)

> *Is any sick among you? let him call for the elders of the church; and let them pray over him, anointing him with oil in the name of the Lord.*
> —*JAMES 5:16*

Question 75: I know someone who is sick. What should I do?

God has a place in his heart for the sick. Because of this, the Word teaches us how to minister to them. If you know someone who is sick:

- Preach healing to them: Tell them that God wants to see them well. This is the Good News — the Gospel! You'd be amazed how many people don't know this or don't believe it. Show them in Scripture where it says God wants to heal them, and help them build their faith in God's healing power (Luke 4:18-19).
- Lay hands on them and anoint them with oil: If they are willing to receive prayer, lay hands on them and anoint them with oil. Expect God to release healing through your hands (James 5:16).
- Keep them encouraged: Don't let them give up on their faith if they do not see an instant result. Text them Scriptures, call them and give God thanks together, share with them testimonies of God's faithfulness, etc. We must always keep one another lifted up during the healing process, because it can often be discouraging (1 Thessalonians 5:11).

Question 76: Why don't some people get healed, even after we pray?

It's likely we've all known someone who did everything they were supposed to do but didn't get healed. They were people of faith but they went to the grave with their sickness. So the question becomes *why didn't they get healed?* And the only answer is *nobody knows*. Some things only God knows (Deuteronomy 29:29) and we have to settle that this is enough. Of course, this is easier said than done. But we can trust that the comfort of the Holy Spirit is able to relieve us, even if we never figure out what happened (2 Corinthians 1:4).

Despite our pain, God asks us to trust him even when life doesn't make sense. And part of trusting him means believing that he is good when the math doesn't seem to add up. We can trust, despite the loss of someone to sickness, that God:

- Desires to heal.
- Is not to blame.
- Loved the person who died.
- Is still faithful to all his promises.

Though we may likely never know why a person didn't receive their healing, we should never doubt what God's Word tells us about God. We never know *all* the details behind a situation, so situations aren't reliable and usually how we perceive the situation isn't either. But we can trust that God's Word is. Therefore, our best bet is to leave the situation in God's hand and praise him anyway. And even during death, there is still much to praise God for, believe it or not.

God's Word declares that Jesus has defeated death. Even if sickness has taken a believer, the believer still wins in the end because there is eternal life in Christ (John 17:3). God has promised that he will one day raise their body from the grave and make it incorruptible, free from the possibility of ever getting sick and dying again:

> *But let me reveal to you a wonderful secret. We will not all die, but we will all be transformed! It will happen in a moment, in the blink of an eye, when the last trumpet is blown. For when the trumpet sounds, those who have died will be raised to live forever. And we who are living will also be transformed. For our dying bodies must be transformed into bodies that will never die; our mortal bodies must be transformed into immortal bodies. Then, when our dying bodies have been transformed into bodies that will never die, this Scripture will be fulfilled: "Death is swallowed up in victory. O death, where is your victory? O death, where is your sting?"*
> —1 CORINTHIANS 15:51-55

While death to sickness may seem like a defeat, in the long run those who die in Christ have the victory. We are more than conquerors and in this we can take comfort and be glad:

> *And I am convinced that nothing can ever separate us from God's love. Neither death nor life, neither angels nor demons, neither our fears for today nor our worries about tomorrow— not even the powers of hell can separate us from God's love.*
> —ROMANS 8:38

CHAPTER 15

What's My Purpose?

Purpose is the reason something is created and the end for which it exists. The purpose of a car is transportation. The purpose of a house is space for living. Frankly, there is nothing that exists that does not have a purpose, including you and me.

So why are we here? People answer that question in various ways: to be a parent, to provide services, to help others. This list can get long and extensive — certainly everyone has different ideas about their lives. While many things can serve as *purposes* for living, to discover *the main purpose,* we must look to the Creator. What was in his mind when he formed us? Why did he decide to make us? What exactly was going on when he reckoned that we should live? Unless we discover the answer to this, our lives will seem empty despite any great accomplishments we make. Just ask King Solomon.

Solomon was a powerful king who enjoyed an excess of life's greatest pleasures. He obtained everything his heart wanted and could say about everything, "been there, done that." But Solomon looked back on his life's accomplishments with bitter sadness. He stated:

> Everything is meaningless," says the Teacher, "completely meaningless!"
> —*ECCLESIASTES 1:2*

How could someone with so much say something like this? Because Solomon wanted something that would last eternally (Ecclesiastes 3:11). We all do. And that's how God wants us to feel because he created us for so much more than just this life. He created us for eternity. And until we take hold of our eternal purpose, everything else will eventually become unfulfilling and empty.

Question 77: What is the meaning of life?

The meaning of life is to know God and to have an ongoing relationship with him. Out of this relationship, God reveals his love and goodness to us, which satisfies the deepest longing of our hearts (1 John 4:8).

The first man, Adam, experienced this. There was a problem, however. Sin entered the world though his choice to disobey God (Romans 5:12). This sin separated the human race from God and smothered its ability to have an ongoing relationship with him. God acted out of his love and sent Jesus to pay for the price of our sins in order that our relationship with him might be restored. Notice:

> *But God showed his great love for us by sending Christ*
> *to die for us while we were still sinners.*
> *—ROMANS 5:8*

Now the meaning of life is found in a relationship with Jesus Christ because, through him, we can enjoy the blessings of his love and goodness again. This is why those who give their lives to Christ always say it comes with joy and peace that they couldn't find elsewhere in the world. Nothing else can give us this relationship with God — not money, not a successful career, not the fulfillment of our ambitions and dreams — only Jesus.

After our relationship with God is restored, there is fulfillment in obeying God. King Solomon admitted this: at the end of his life he said that there is no pleasure like pleasing God. Notice:

> *That's the whole story. Here now is my final conclusion: Fear*
> *God and obey his commands, for this is everyone's duty.*
> *—ECCLESIASTES 12:13-14*

How invigorating to think that we are living to please the eternal judge of the universe rather than just a manager, supervisor, or a girlfriend or boyfriend? Living for eternity is living on a mission.

Finally, God has a unique plan for all of us. This can be discovered in the gifting that God has equipped us with. What's your gift? What do you excel at? Certainly, God has given each of us something special:

> *In his grace, God has given us different gifts for doing certain things well.*
> *—ROMANS 12:6*

God hasn't given you a gift merely to make money or just to improve your standard of living. Your gift was given to you in order serve the Lord and fulfill his vision for your life. Using your gift this way will not only bring abundance in this life, but in the life to come (Matthew 6:19-21). So give your gift unto the Lord's service and watch your life start to make more sense:

> *God has given each of you a gift from his great variety of*
> *spiritual gifts. Use them well to serve one another.*
> *—1 PETER 4:10*

Question 78: What can I do to help God?

It should be our desire to help God accomplish his purposes in the earth, so much so that we are driven by what he wants and not necessarily what we want. Like Christ, our attitude should always be:

> *Yet I want your will to be done, not mine.*
> —*MATTHEW 26:39*

It might be easy to say we want this, but the rubber meets the road when it comes time to deliver with our actions. If we really have a heart for God, we will want to help him *all the time* — not just when it's convenient for us. There will be plenty of times when it is a tremendous inconvenience to help God out. It might mean sacrificing our time, being ridiculed and made fun of, feeling awkward, or giving something up that we might have really wanted for ourselves. But helping God never means losing out. God always returns our service to him in a big way (Luke 6:38).

Helping God out begins with obedience. There are endless things that God may ask you to do, but all of them require saying *yes* to him. And it is important to say *yes* to God because everything he asks us to do is extremely important — it is going toward leading people to him! We are ministers of reconciliation. God uses us to help people find his delivering, saving, and healing power. Notice:

> *So we are Christ's ambassadors; God is making his appeal through us. We speak for Christ when we plead, "Come back to God!"*
> —*2 CORINTHIANS 5:21*

Here are some things we must always do to be of service to God:

- Be available: No matter where or when, we should be ready to spring to action if God says. Whether at the office, on vacation, or in the middle of the night, we must be always be ready (2 Timothy 4:2).
- Pray and intercede: Prayer changes the course of things because it is an invitation for God to have his way (1 Thessalonians 5:17).
- Stand up for righteousness: Vote for righteous candidates, help righteous causes, and stand against injustices.
- Take care of the poor: God tells us that the less fortunate have a special place in his heart. God takes care of those who take care of the poor (Proverbs 19:17).
- Respect your authorities: Rebellion is a horrible sin that aggravates God. Our earthly leaders are an extension of God's authority, therefore, he asks us to obey them. The only exception is if they are trying to force us to do something against the will of God (Romans 13:1).

- Avail yourself to church leaders: Every Christian should serve in their home church and do what their church leadership asks of them, with a cheerful heart (Psalm 100:2).
- Raise a godly family: Decide that your home will serve God — take your family to church, give your children a Christian education, don't allow anything in your home that displeases the Lord (Joshua 24:15).

Question 79: What does being a servant mean?

While Jesus lived, he was a servant: he was completely devoted to helping others, even at the expense of his own will. He said:

> *For even the Son of Man came not to be served but to serve others and to give his life as a ransom for many.*
> *—MATTHEW 20:28*

A servant is one who does not live for themselves. They are genuinely concerned about other people; they invest their time and energy into others, and place them first. Because Jesus lives in us, this is how we should be:

> *Don't be selfish; don't try to impress others. Be humble, thinking of others as better than yourselves.*
> *—PHILIPPIANS 2:3*

God actually created us to be servants. In fact, serving is the path to greatness in the Kingdom of God:

> *The greatest among you must be a servant.*
> *—MATTHEW 23:11*

In other words, no matter how known or unknown we are in the world, servanthood makes us great in the eyes of God. The Lord never forgets our acts of service and is going to reward us for them (Matthew 25:21-23).

The opposite of being a servant is living selfishly. But God warned us that selfishness causes a lonely, unfulfilled life. After all, the whole reason man was separated from God was because of his selfish desires (Genesis 3).

So if we want to be great in the Kingdom of God, we have to put away selfishness and be a servant the Lord. And in order to be a *good* servant of the Lord, we should:

- Serve without expecting anything in return.
- Serve without expecting recognition from others.

- Not be motivated by personal agendas.
- Be faithful and committed.
- Serve with gladness and humility.

When we live like this, we will discover the joy of serving an eternal purpose.

CHAPTER 16

Where Is This Crazy World Heading?

There's a lot going on in the world today, to say the least. People have become *anxious*. Some of the questions they ask are: Where is the technology boom leading us? Will a rogue government ever decide to use nuclear weapons? Have traditional values been lost forever? Every human shares the same concern for the future because the future seems largely uncertain.

However, Jesus told us not to fear. Though it might seem unclear to us, he has everything under control. As a matter of fact, God actually told us to anticipate the future with joy. How can that be possible? Because it is in God's hands (Psalm 31:15). No matter how large or threatening a situation, disaster, or government becomes, it is not greater than God, and it cannot stop his plan for the future. We are safe in God's hand and this should give us overwhelming confidence, no matter what the news media reports:

> *Yes, and the Lord will deliver me from every evil attack and will bring me safely into his heavenly Kingdom. All glory to God forever and ever! Amen.*
> *—2 Timothy 4:18*

Question 80: What is God's plan for the future?

God's ultimate plan for the future is the total establishment of his government upon the earth. His government is known throughout Scripture as the Kingdom of God. When Jesus came the first time, he declared that his Kingdom had broken into human history:

> *Jesus traveled throughout the region of Galilee, teaching in the synagogues and announcing the Good News about the Kingdom. And he healed every kind of disease and illness.*
> *—Matthew 4:23*

He also declared that his coming was not the total coming of the Kingdom nor the full establishment of his government. He said that part of his Kingdom was yet to come (Matthew

6:10). And until it does, the sons and daughters of the Kingdom (you and I) must live in this age, intermingled with the wicked. This is illustrated by Jesus's parable of the tares and wheat (Matthew 13:24-29).

Jesus promised that, at some point, he would come again, set up his earthly reign, and fully establish his government. Those who are part of his Kingdom when he comes will rule with him. And this Kingdom will persist forever:

> *The world has now become the Kingdom of our Lord and*
> *of his Christ, and he will reign forever and ever."*
> —*REVELATION 11:15*

When this happens, Jesus will judge the wicked (Matthew 13:47), rule over every nation (Revelation 1:5), and the glory of his Kingdom will cover the earth (Isaiah 1:9). All ethnicities will belong to God, and there will be no threat of any enemy. This present and corrupt earth will be purified through fire and the curse of sin will be lifted. Truly, a new world and perfect community await (2 Peter 3:10-13).

We must place our faith in God's plan. Instead of putting our hope in the unstable plans of human governments, we should place it in Christ and anticipate our future place in his Kingdom. We do this by:

- Denying the sinful enticements of this world (Titus 2:12).
- Persevering during suffering (2 Timothy 2:3-5).
- Enduring criticism and persecution (no matter how intense) from those who don't believe (2 Timothy 3:12).
- Praying for Jesus to come again (Matthew 6:10).

Question 81: When is Jesus coming back?

People often wonder, *Are we living in the last days?* especially when a significant political event or tragedy takes place. Interestingly enough, the Bible tells us that not only are we living in the last days now but that we have been living in the last days since the first coming of Christ. Notice:

> *And now in these final days, he has spoken to us through his*
> *Son. God promised everything to the Son as an inheritance,*
> *and through the Son he created the universe.*
> —*HEBREWS 1:2*

The term *last days* refers to the period of time before this age comes to an end and the reign of Christ begins. As we get closer to the coming of Christ, these last days will be earmarked by deeper tension and trouble. God's Word says that society will become increasingly sinful:

You should know this, Timothy, that in the last days there will be very difficult times. For people will love only themselves and their money. They will be boastful and proud, scoffing at God, disobedient to their parents, and ungrateful. They will consider nothing sacred. They will be unloving and unforgiving; they will slander others and have no self-control. They will be cruel and hate what is good. They will betray their friends, be reckless, be puffed up with pride, and love pleasure rather than God. They will act religious, but they will reject the power that could make them godly. Stay away from people like that!
–2 TIMOTHY 3:1-5

We see this occurring today, particularly in the United States of America. America is of special concern because for the last 300 years it has been considered the moral hub of the world. Now, with the moral hub eroding, righteousness is becoming all the more disdained:

Jesus also told us that false prophets would rise up between his first and second coming:

For false messiahs and false prophets will rise up and perform signs and wonders so as to deceive, if possible, even God's chosen ones.
—MARK 13:22

Consider all of the cults, false religions, and deceptive sects that have formed since the time Christ said this.

Jesus also warned of political upheavals (Matthew 24:7), wars (Matthew 24:6), natural disasters (Matthew 24:7), and hatred for those following him (Matthew 24:9). The more frequently these take place, the closer we know we are to his coming. Considering that Jesus warned us that we are in the last days over 2000 years ago, and considering how often these events are taking place now (every day), we can safely conclude that we are now living in the last *hour* before his coming and reign.

Although Jesus told us that nobody knows the exact moment he will come (Matthew 24:36), we can use the signs of the age to discern that we are close to his arrival:

Now concerning how and when all this will happen, dear brothers and sisters, we don't really need to write you. For you know quite well that the day of the Lord's return will come unexpectedly, like a thief in the night. When people are saying, "Everything is peaceful and secure," then disaster will fall on them as suddenly as a pregnant woman's labor pains begin. And there will be no escape. But you aren't in the dark about these things, dear brothers and sisters, and you won't be surprised when the day of the Lord comes like a thief.
–1 THESSALONIANS 5:1-4

Question 82: If Jesus can come at any time, what should I do?

Jesus tells us that we must be prepared for his coming. This is what he expects of us. Notice:

> *You also must be ready all the time, for the Son of*
> *Man will come when least expected.*
> —*MATTHEW 24:44*

The apostle Paul later echoed Jesus and said:

> *So be on your guard, not asleep like the others. Stay alert and be clearheaded.*
> *Night is the time when people sleep and drinkers get drunk. But let us*
> *who live in the light be clearheaded, protected by the armor of faith and*
> *love, and wearing as our helmet the confidence of our salvation.*
> —*1 THESSALONIANS 5:6-7*

In order to be prepared, we should:

- Live holy: Whatever we do should be done with the thought that *Jesus could come back while I'm doing this.* This simple consideration should govern our character and practices.
- Remain committed: Our allegiance to Christ should be more than one foot in and one foot out, especially during difficult times. Christ must be our everything.
- Stay focused: The attractions of the world will come to compete for our attention and turn our focus away from doing the will of God. This is something we must resist by keeping God's Word before our eyes.
- Tell the world that Jesus is coming: Jesus is coming to judge the world, so now is the time for people to accept his mercy and grace. Therefore, we must let them know, now (John 9:4).
- Do your best doing what God has called you to do: God has a unique plan and purpose for each person who serves him. Excelling at this helps God's Kingdom.

CHAPTER 17

What Does God Think About...

Social issues, or *hot button issues*, are the most sensitive things to discuss today. This is because they are controversial and when something is controversial, it involves people's emotions. Our stance on these represents our worldview or our outlook on life. Hearing someone disagree means hearing someone say that we are wrong. And that's moving.

As Christians, before we take a side on an issue, it's vital that we are willing to make the Word of God our authority. We should trust what God has to say above what we've been taught at home, at the university, or through life experience. What God says is more important than our perceptions of injustice, our personal experience, other people's experience, and accounts of horror.

Putting God's Word first might mean refiguring some things, possibly switching sides on where we stand. But being a Christian means absolute surrender to God's Word, even if it means laying down some of our strongest views in order to arm ourselves with God's. If we believe that God is totally good, then we should have no qualms about taking his side, even if it makes us seem unpopular or out of touch with what society calls *progress*. This is part of renewing our minds:

> *Don't copy the behavior and customs of this world, but let God transform*
> *you into a new person by changing the way you think. Then you will learn*
> *to know God's will for you, which is good and pleasing and perfect.*
> —ROMANS 12:2

Question 83: Are we supposed to tolerate homosexuality?

There is no doubt that many homosexuals are kind, talented, and productive members of society. God loves them tremendously and they should not be treated with any less dignity, respect, or honor than any other person in society. Hate crimes against them are atrocious. Nobody who harms homosexuals represents Christ or is doing as Scripture teaches. Christ tells us to love our neighbor as ourselves (Mark 12:31) and even to love those we consider an enemy (Matthew 5:44). There is just no excuse for treating gays harshly for being gay.

With that said, the next thing we need to do is look at what God's Word says about the *act* of homosexuality. The New Testament says the following:

> *That is why God abandoned them to their shameful desires. Even the women turned against the natural way to have sex and instead indulged in sex with each other. And the men, instead of having normal sexual relations with women, burned with lust for each other. Men did shameful things with other men, and as a result of this sin, they suffered within themselves the penalty they deserved.*
> —ROMANS 1:26-27

> *Don't you realize that those who do wrong will not inherit the Kingdom of God? Don't fool yourselves. Those who indulge in sexual sin, or who worship idols, or commit adultery, or are male prostitutes, or practice homosexuality, or are thieves, or greedy people, or drunkards, or are abusive, or cheat people—none of these will inherit the Kingdom of God.*
> —1 CORINTHIANS 6:9-10

> *For the law was not intended for people who do what is right. It is for people who are lawless and rebellious, who are ungodly and sinful, who consider nothing sacred and defile what is holy, who kill their father or mother or commit other murders. The law is for people who are sexually immoral, or who practice homosexuality, or are slave traders, liars, promise breakers, or who do anything else that contradicts the wholesome teaching that comes from the glorious Good News entrusted to me by our blessed God.*
> —1 TIMOTHY 1:9-11

Clearly, God's Word teaches that homosexual behavior is sinful and displeasing to the Lord. If our Creator is displeased with it, clearly he didn't make anyone homosexual from birth. In fact, science has not been able to prove that homosexuality is genetic. Homosexuality is a behavior that is acted upon by choice, regardless of what leads a person to make the choice to act. The act of homosexuality is categorized with other behaviors that are done through willful choice, such as sex before marriage, adultery, lying, getting drunk, and being greedy. Like all sin, God calls those who are involved with homosexuality to repent and turn to him for forgiveness, otherwise they will not enter Heaven.

Is this discrimination against homosexuality? Absolutely not. God didn't just single out homosexuality as the only sin he will judge; he included *all* sin. To God, all sin is wrong and must be turned from in order to receive eternal life. Those of us who have repented and turned to God should exhort others to do the same. We shouldn't do this in a condemning and forceful way, but with an appeal from concern.

As Christians, our responsibility is two-fold: we must love homosexuals and treat them as kindly as we would anyone else who is living a life of sin, and we must be willing to speak the truth in love when it affects us, even when it means being criticized and called a bigot. You see, today there is a movement among homosexuals (not all, but many) to force their way of life to be taught as core education. This means teaching our kids that homosexuality is not wrong — that it is perfectly fine and natural. God's Word clearly says otherwise. Therefore, we have a responsibility to respectfully oppose it.

Because of legislation that has passed and the decline of morality within society, opposing homosexuality often causes acute persecution and bitter anger toward the person opposing it. Disagreeing with the homosexual agenda is almost certain to get you accused of trying to stop people from being happy. But be as it may, we must remember that our purpose in life is to fear God, not man (Matthew 10:28).

Question 84: Does the Bible degrade women and put them down?

It's said by some that the Bible degrades women, making them less than men. In other words, the Bible is often accused of teaching misogyny. Because it is a book from antiquity, some don't think it is with the times. But it's God's Word; if anyone honors and respects women, it's God. After all, woman was his idea (Genesis 2:18-22).

One of the greatest accusations brought against the Bible in the name of misogyny is Ephesians 5:22, which says:

> *For wives, this means submit to your husbands as to the Lord. For a husband is the head of his wife as Christ is the head of the church. He is the Savior of his body, the church. As the church submits to Christ, so you wives should submit to your husbands in everything.*
> —*EPHESIANS 5:22*

Yet, this couldn't possibly mean that the Bible is teaching men to dominate their wives or that, somehow, husbands are more important than their wives because the next verses says:

> *For husbands, this means love your wives, just as Christ loved the church. He gave up his life for her to make her holy and clean, washed by the cleansing of God's word. He did this to present her to himself as a glorious church without a spot or wrinkle or any other blemish. Instead, she will be holy and without fault. In the same way, husbands ought to love their wives as they love their own bodies. For a man who loves his wife actually shows love for himself. No one hates his own body but feeds and cares for it, just as Christ cares for the church.*
> —*EPHESIANS 5:25-28*

Together, these verses teach an awesome agreement between the husband and the wife. The wife is to help her husband and the husband is to serve his wife. And not only is the husband supposed to *just* serve his wife, he is to serve her the same way that Christ served the Church — through total sacrifice. Man is supposed to put his wife ahead of himself, preferring her always. This is how he leads through love. This is about as far from misogyny as it gets, folks.

There are other examples in the Bible that show just how valuable women are. For instance:

- Jesus saved a woman guilty of adultery from those trying to harm her (John 8:9-11).
- Jesus had a close and respectful relationship with women, such as Mary and Martha (Luke 10:38-42).
- Jesus ministered to the woman at the well even though it was socially unacceptable at the time (John 4:9-10).
- There were many women converts in the Early Church (Acts 8:12).
- Women were used by God in ministry (Philippians 4:3).

The only way the Bible can be accused of misogyny is if people take Scriptures and twist them, making them say something the Bible never intended. Of course, there are acts of misogyny *described* in the Bible (Judges 19:25-29). However, the Bible never endorses them. In fact, it condemns them. God values women as equals with men and he expects us to do the same:

> *There is no longer Jew or Gentile, slave or free, male and*
> *female. For you are all one in Christ Jesus.*
> —GALATIANS 3:28

Question 85: Does life begin at conception, or birth, or somewhere in between?

In order to address the topic of abortion, we must first answer the question of when life begins. Many scientists say it begins at conception, others say it doesn't. It's likely this debate will carry on into the 21st century. We, however, can look to God's Word for a definitive answer. And God's Word declares that *life begins at conception*. Notice these Scriptures which make it very clear that God values human life while it is in the womb:

> *Listen to me, all you in distant lands! Pay attention, you who are far away!*
> *The Lord called me before my birth; from within the womb he called me by*
> *name…And now the Lord speaks—the one who formed me in my mother's*
> *womb to be his servant, who commissioned me to bring Israel back to him.*
> —ISAIAH 49:1,5

> *I knew you before I formed you in your mother's womb. Before you were*
> *born I set you apart and appointed you as my prophet to the nations.*
> —JEREMIAH 1:5

You made all the delicate, inner parts of my body and
knit me together in my mother's womb.
—PSALM 139:13

God says that he calls us, forms us, appoints us, and knits us…all before we are born. Abortion, then, is not only destroying the body of a baby, it is terminating the calling and appointment that God had set upon it. This is no different than murder. And murder is a very serious sin.

On the political side of this question, pro-choice advocates stand for a woman's right to choose whether or not she wants to carry her baby until birth. They believe that it is unconstitutional for the government to tell women what to do with their bodies. However, the government has the responsibility of protecting life, liberty, and the pursuit of happiness for all life — even if that life is still unborn. Therefore, the government *should* intervene and stop women from executing an innocent life that is precious to God, especially a life that cannot defend itself.

The choice concerning childbirth should come before intercourse happens. Those who choose to engage in sex should do so fully aware that God created intercourse for the purpose of reproduction. Participating in it holds likely chances of conception. When conception occurs, the choice has already been made, and a life has been conceived. Aborting it is not an acceptable means of birth control. God's design for birth control is self-control.

Of course, there are very touchy aspects of abortion, such as in the case of rape. While rape is horrific and tragic, should it result in pregnancy a life still has been conceived, and God still values it. Abortion cannot be the answer. God will honor a woman for being courageous and strong and carrying the baby until birth — even if she gives it up for adoption. God will give her grace and strength and will reward her for giving life a chance.

Final Thought

Dear Friend—
If these questions have done their job properly, they have not only provided you with solid answers, they have inspired more questions to on go with from here. Use these questions to continue your studies. Search for answers, dig deep, and don't give up. The harder you search, the more wisdom you will find, and the more your life will be enriched.

And don't ever be afraid to ask a question you may have. If scientists didn't ask questions, we'd never have our modern cures. If physicists never asked questions, we would never have put a man on the moon. If engineers never asked questions, our skylines wouldn't exist. And if you don't keep asking questions, you may miss out on some of the most phenomenal insights that God has for your life.

Remember, questions are keys that will unlock where you have never been. Use them, use them, use them:

> *Keep on asking, and you will receive what you ask for. Keep on seeking, and you will find. Keep on knocking, and the door will be opened to you. For everyone who asks, receives. Everyone who seeks, finds. And to everyone who knocks, the door will be opened.*
> —MATTHEW 7:7-8

62120776R00072

Made in the USA
Lexington, KY
30 March 2017